'OLD ST PAUL'S'

The Society of Antiquaries'
Diptych, 1616

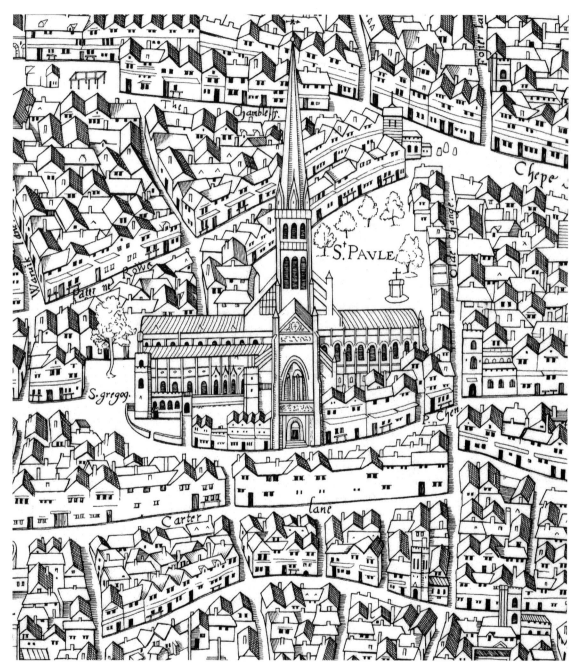

Frontispiece.   The plate from the Dessau section of the Copperplate map, showing the medieval Cathedral, its magnificent spire still intact, before 1561.
Museum of London

'OLD ST PAUL'S'
The Society of Antiquaries'
Diptych, 1616

By
PAMELA TUDOR-CRAIG
with Christopher Whittick

Edited by
Penelope Hunting
and
Ann Saunders

London Topographical Society
Publication No. 163
and
The Society of Antiquaries of London

2004

Publication No. 163 of the
London Topographical Society
3 Meadway Gate, London NW11

ISBN 0 902087 50 9

PRODUCED IN GREAT BRITAIN BY
OUTSET SERVICES LTD, CLIFFORD, NR LEEDS

CONTENTS

Dedication   vi

Foreword by Richard Chartres, Bishop of London   vii

'Old St Paul's'   1

Acknowledgements   34

Notes   34

Topographical and historical notes by Ann Saunders   40

Appendix 1 – *The Complaint of Paules*   43

Appendix 2 – *Portland-Stone in Paules-Church-yard*   61

Colour plates are to be found between pp. 12 and 13

For
Roy Strong

FOREWORD

Fund-raising is a truly ecumenical subject and a matter of perennial concern for those who have the care of great buildings like St Paul's Cathedral. At the moment of writing, the contemporary St Paul's is engaged in a vast cleaning operation and is appealing for substantial funds to endow its future work.

In this study of 'Old St Paul's', the diptych in the possession of the Society of Antiquaries of London, Pamela Tudor-Craig gives us a glimpse of a time in the first quarter of the seventeenth century when the Cathedral was in an especially dilapidated condition. She introduces us to the kind of loyal layman upon whom all fund-raising efforts depend, Henry Farley the Scrivener, a visionary freeman, of whom the modern Company can be very proud. His diptych, commissioned from John Gipkyn, was part of Farley's campaign to solicit aid for the battered shrine by presenting a 'before' and 'after' view of St Paul's. Strangely he encountered indifference and even hostility as a result of his efforts.

Fund-raising sermons do not have today the efficacy which was attributed to them in the seventeenth century. The diptych of 1616 pictures a sermon being preached at St Paul's Cross in the presence of the King. Life followed art, and James I did in fact come in 1620 to hear my predecessor Bishop King preach on the text, 'Thou shalt arise and have mercy upon Sion ... for thy servants take pleasure in her stones and favour the dust thereof'. The translation of Psalm 102 is taken from the newly published Authorized Version rather than from the Book of Common Prayer.

James described the Bishop as 'the King of Preachers', and it is interesting to see how he sought to convince his congregation in a sermon which in its printed version extends to fifty-one pages. There is a frank appeal to civic pride, 'the forrest of masts' upon the river, whose 'cleansing', the Bishop hopes, 'will follow in good time'. Biblical citation, classical allusion and comparison with the competitive marvels of contemporary European cities are assembled in a rhetorical symphony of a kind destined to fade as the century wore on and as a more analytical style of biblical exposition took its place.

The printed version survives in numerous copies, but it is unclear how effective it was at the time. St Paul's had to wait until the appointment of the energetic William Laud as Bishop of London before anything much was achieved in a campaign overseen by Inigo Jones.

We are much indebted to Pamela Tudor-Craig for doing belated justice to Henry Farley and illuminating the sequence of events which ensured the survival of the diptych. High art is cherished from generation to generation, whereas fund-raising ephemera are commonly rapidly discarded. We are fortunate that John Gipkyn's panels have come down to us and that, in a year when St Paul's celebrates its 1400th anniversary, fresh light has been shed on a fascinating part of the story of the Cathedral.

✠ Richard

The Rt Revd & Rt Hon. Richard Chartres DD FSA
Bishop of London

'OLD ST PAUL'S'
THE SOCIETY OF ANTIQUARIES' DIPTYCH, 1616

By PAMELA TUDOR-CRAIG

THE diptych, known popularly as 'Old St Paul's', is a large painting on two hinged wooden panels (col. pls. I–III). When closed, the outer cover shows a royal procession on its way from Southwark to St Paul's Cathedral. The inner panels represent on the left hand a preaching scene outside the Cathedral, shown in its early seventeenth-century state of disrepair, and on the right, a vision of the building, newly restored, its rebuilt spire ringed about by soaring, singing angels. Each leaf, gable-shaped, measures four feet two inches by three feet four inches. There does not appear to be any record of the actual arrival of the picture at the Society of Antiquaries, an event which must have taken place early in 1781.[1] On 30 May 1780 a committee of the Society had been formed to deal with the furnishing of their new rooms at Somerset House and their first meeting in their new premises was on 11 January 1781.[2] There was nowhere the Society could have accommodated so large a picture before that date.

A full description of the diptych first reached the reading public through the pages of the *Gentleman's Magazine* for April 1780, where an anonymous contributor wrote:

> This painting was for many years in the family of the Tookes, of whom three had been successively rectors of Lamborne in Essex, from 1704 to 1776. On the decease of the late Rector it was purchased as a neglected piece of furniture, which had never quitted the attic, for a few shillings, by Mr. Webster, a surgeon at Chigwell, who is the present proprietor.[3]

It is probable the Society of Antiquaries was alerted to the painting's existence by Michael Tyson, FSA, who succeeded the three Tookes as rector of Lambourne in 1778, only to die two years later. Richard Gough, Director of the Society, and his friend, John Nichols, who would engrave the processional panel of the diptych for his *Progresses of King James the First* (fig. 1), took part in the transaction.

At a meeting of the Society on 2 May 1782 Mr Owen Salusbury Brereton presented a copy of the sermon relating to the diptych — which was by that date in the library at Somerset House. The Minutes record Brereton's gift of:

> a sermon accidently picked up by him, preached by Bishop King in 1620 at St Paul's Cross before King James I ... One Henry Farley, zealous for church-work, and the rather as being a Projector, made all sorts of Applications by Plans, Proposals and Petitions, to the City, and even to the Court, for contributions to set up a new steeple: among other Devices he got a Painting made by one John Gripkin [*sic*] from which Prints were taken, and dispersed, representing a new Steeple, & various other ornaments of his own Projecting, wch. Painting is now the Property of this Society and is in their Library...[4]

THE PROVENANCE OF THE ST PAUL'S DIPTYCH

It might be assumed that the history of the diptych has been uneventful since its arrival at the Society's house at the beginning of 1781, but that is not entirely the

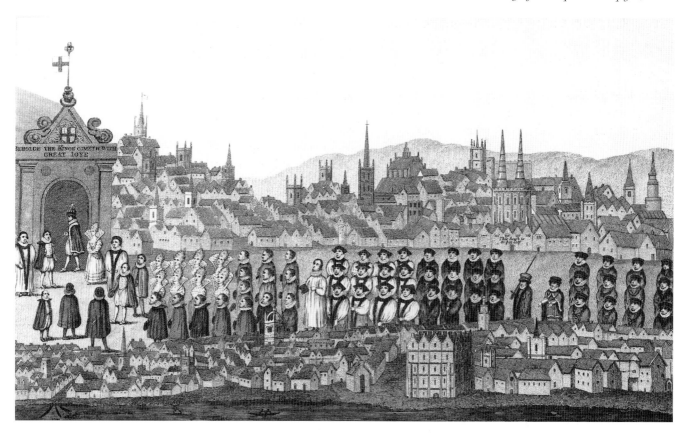

Figure 1.   The procession from the outer cover of the diptych engraved for the frontispiece of John Nichols' *Progresses of King James the First,* IV, 1828.
Society of Antiquaries of London

case. In March 1790 the President, Lord Leicester, ordered on a motion that Lady Lucan...

> be permitted to have at her house the old painting in the Library of this Society representing Dr Shaw preaching at St Paul's Cross, in order to take a Copy of the Same.[5]

Margaret Bingham, Countess of Lucan, who died in 1818, was an amateur painter whose *magnum opus* was the illustration of Shakespeare's historical plays in five volumes.[6] It would appear that within nine years of the Society's acquisition of the diptych, the significance of its contents were already misunderstood, since Dr. Shaw's sermon had, in fact, been delivered on 22 June 1483, in support of the future Richard III's claim to the throne. When Lady Lucan returned the diptych it was placed in the basement at Somerset House. Nichols complained in 1828:

> Grieved I am to add that it is now consigned, with several other pictures and curiosities at various times presented to the Society, to a subterranean warehouse. It is to be hoped that space may soon be procured for displaying the many treasures the Society possesses. As it is presents are totally discouraged from those that have been made being never exhibited.[7]

The Society may never again have found room to display the diptych at Somerset House. The picture was catalogued there by Albert Way in 1847[8] and by George Scharf in 1865.[9] Scharf, the first Director of the National Portrait Gallery, brought much scholarship to bear. He identified the figures on the idealized spire as, reading from the bottom upwards, Prince Charles and Queen Anne; the King alone and two smaller figures, apparently Lord Darnley and Mary Queen of Scots.

When the Society moved to Burlington House over Christmas and New Year 1874–5, the space on the first landing of the staircase was found to fit the picture as it was at that time disposed. That is to say, the diptych was displayed open, with the renovated spire on the left-hand side, and the preaching scene to the right. The procession was therefore on the back of the right-hand panel, and with caution it could be seen occasionally. However, the existence of the procession scene on the reverse was so little known that, when the picture went to the 'Artists' Quarters' exhibition at the Museum of London in 2001, the special case made for its display had a solid back, prohibiting the display of what is to many its most interesting aspect.

When the picture was studied and cleaned by Simon Gillespie in 2000–1 it was found that the hinges had been altered. The painting was reading back to front. It must start, closed, with the procession, proceed when opened to the preaching scene, and conclude with the new spire. The mistake in the disposition must have been made in or before 1780, for the panels were meticulously described in the 'wrong' order before they came to the Society.[10]

As the *Gentleman's Magazine* tells us, the diptych had belonged to the Tookes, which gives it a pedigree going back to 1707. But why should the Tookes of Lambourne in Essex have owned it in the first place? The answer lies in the chancel of their church, where memorials to John Winniffe of Sherbourne (d. 1630) and his son Thomas, rector from 1608 to 1641, are to be found. The son has a wall memorial on the north of the chancel, where we learn of:

> a death not private but public, almost the decease of the Church of England (unless God forestalls it): Thomas Winniffus, Doctor of Sacred Theology, honey-sweet speaker, vigorous in teaching, judicious in refutation, personally respectful in rebuke, persuasive in exhortation, well-liked by his prince, dear to him and on familiar terms with him, beloved of the nobility, delight of the clergy, revered by citizens and people. Neither royal palace nor Bishop's residence, nor great city, nor private country estate, nor the age itself hath seen anyone more virtuous than he: I mourn such a man when so greatly do we want and lack good men in this (which is to be) reckoned the worst of times.

Thomas Winniffe was a royal chaplain. In 1608 he became rector of Lambourne, where he brought his father to live. He became Dean of St Paul's in 1631, and when in 1641 he became Bishop of Lincoln he was allowed to retain the appointment at St Paul's but resigned his Lambourne living. In that year his house in Westminster was destroyed by a mob. In November 1646 all Bishops' lands were vested in trustees for the benefit of the Commonwealth. In the same year Winniffe bought the advowson of Lambourne and lived there until his death in 1654. Thomas Winniffe, therefore, had reason to bring with him to Lambourne what he could salvage of the Church's property. The rectory where he and his successors lived still stands and it has plenty of tall attics where 'politically incorrect' items could be stored. Here, it seems, the diptych lay undisturbed from 1646 until it was rediscovered soon after the death of the last Tooke rector of Lambourne in 1776.

In entering upon the Deanery of St Paul's in 1631 Winniffe inherited from his predecessor a third of his religious manuscripts, and a picture called 'the Skeleton' which hung in the hall. That predecessor was Dr John Donne, appointed in 1621. Donne's will of 13 December 1630, proved on 5 April 1631, mentions a number of pictures, some of them surprising in the house of a Protestant clergyman.[11] His painting of the Blessed Virgin was left to the Earl of Carlisle, the Magdalene in his study went to George Garrard, the Blessed Virgin and Joseph went to Dr Brooke, Master of Trinity, and the Entombment in his study to the Earl of Kent. Quite distinct from these were items which were to remain in place in his house, including 'four large pictures of the four great prophets which hang in the hall, and that large picture of ancient churchwork which hangs in the lobby leading to my chamber'. Here, surely, outside Donne's chamber hung the diptych, until Dean Winniffe smuggled it away from the Cromwellian soldiery in 1646.

So we are able to follow the history of our painting back certainly to 1630, and almost certainly substantially further. Whether it had been given to John Donne, or to Donne's predecessor as Dean, Valentine Carey, or whether, as seems more likely, an official at Whitehall Palace thought the Deanery the most suitable depository for the cumbersome piece left on his hands in the early part of 1617, is not known, but the missing link is very short. It is striking that, despite its proximity and its many inscriptions, John Donne does not seem to have realized what his 'large picture of ancient churchwork' was about, or that it was not in fact in his day ancient. He cannot have given it more than a passing glance. This is an argument in favour of his having found it in the Deanery when he arrived. Nor, in Donne's many sermons, do we find much evidence of his having assumed responsibility for the message of this picture, the repair of St Paul's, initiated just as he entered the Deanery.[12]

Donne seems to have associated churches, as buildings, with death. In sermon 30 for the Countess of Bedford at Harrington House, in January 1621, he said:

> and when we meet in a church, God hath made many echoes, many testimonies of our death in the walls, and in the windows, and he only knows, whether he will make another testimony of our mortality, of the youngest among us, before we part, and make the very place of our burial our deathbed.[13]

This tendency reached its climax in Donne's last sermon, *Death's Duel*, delivered at Whitehall in February 1631, two months before his death.[14] Upon the actual structural members of a Cathedral he built an elaborate metaphor:

> These three considerations, our deliverance *a morte, in morte, per mortem*, from death, in death and by death will abundantly do all the offices of the foundations, of the buttresses, of the contignation [by which he means the knitting together, visibly the flying buttresses] of this our building.

THE COMPOSITION OF THE DIPTYCH

Like a book, the painting tells a story. It displays on the 'cover' a procession. When opened, it shows that procession's destination, a sermon preached from Paul's Cross outside the Cathedral, and in the last panel, the fulfilment of the vision described in that sermon: the central spire of the Cathedral rebuilt and the refurbishment of the whole. So the picture is intended to be 'read' and acted upon.

The long procession on the outside threads its way from St Mary Overie, Southwark,[15] across old London Bridge, along Cheapside, to the threshold of St Paul's Churchyard (col. pl. I). At its head King James I, Queen Anne, and Charles, Prince of Wales, flanked by two dignitaries of the church, are moving through the third of a series of triumphal arches (col. pl. IVA).[16] In the top right-hand corner, looming behind the prospect of London, is a mountain, towards the base of which is a largely erased inscription in capital letters, which appears to read:

MY CARE IS TO THY SELF (col. pl. IVB). The sentiment must be attributed to the small figure in a tall black hat who leans over the top of the mountain, and the purpose of the scene is to represent Henry Farley and to proclaim his identification with the plight of the Cathedral.

Open the diptych, and you are confronted with the company reassembled to hear a sermon delivered at Paul's Cross, the medieval outdoor preaching cross within the angle of the chancel and north transept (col. pl. II).[17] The Cathedral is shown as dark and dilapidated, and shorn of the famous spire which had been struck by lightning in 1561. The eye then travels to the last panel, where a gleaming Cathedral is painted from a higher view-point, giving pride of place to an architectural confection containing statues of James I and his family surmounting the central tower (col pl. III).

The three paintings are ringed about with inscriptions drawn from the Old Testament.[18] The procession has a passage from 2 Chronicles xxiv verses 4, 5 and 9:

> And when it came into the King's mind to renew the house of the Lord, he assembled the Priests and Levites, and said unto them, Go into the cities of Judah, and gather of all Israel money to repair the house of God from yeare to yeare, and hasten the thing; and they made a proclamation throughout Judah and Jerusalem.

Round the preaching scene the border inscription is taken from Haggai in verses 2–3:

> Then speaketh the Lord of Hosts saying, This people say the time is not yet come that the Lord's house should be built. Is it time for you (O yee) to dwell in your seilled houses, and this house lie waste. It is written, my house is the house of prayer.[19]

The vision of a restored St Paul's is surrounded by a passage from Ezra, vii, verse 27:

> Blessed be the Lord God of our Fathers, which putteth such things as these into the heart of our good King, to beautify the house of the Lord.[20]
>
> *Vivat, vincet, regnatque Jacobus.* Amen.

The inscription around the procession on the first panel also carries a coda with the words:

> *Amore, veritate et reverentia.* So invented and at my cost made for me
> H. Farley. 1616. Wrought by John Gipkym. Fiat voluntate Dei.

So we have the author of the scheme, Henry Farley, the artist, John Gipkyn, the intended recipient of the message, James I, and the date.

HENRY FARLEY, 1575–AFTER 1622

What can we find out about the author of *The Complaint of Paules*? He was baptized, as Harry Farley, at East Grinstead in Sussex on 28 May 1575, the last of the six children of John Farley and his wife Clemence to be christened in that parish.[21] When Henry was admitted to the London Scriveners' Company in 1606 he was to describe his father as a tailor, and there seems little doubt that John Farley followed that trade; in 1564 he occupied a burgage-tenement on the north side of East Grinstead market-place, adjoining the mansion of the borough's patron Sir Richard Sackville.[22]

It is also undoubtedly the case that John Farley was an Anglican clergyman. On 24 February 1570, during a vacancy in the diocese of Chichester, he was ordained deacon by Edmund Grindal, the Bishop of London, and Richard Curteys,

Bishop of Chichester, ordained him priest on 9 November 1572; there is evidence that he performed some clerical duties at East Grinstead during his three remaining years in the parish.[23] On 5 November 1576 John Farley was presented to the living of Clayton with the chapel of Keymer, to which he was inducted on 15 December. John and Clemence had at least three more children after the move from East Grinstead.[24] We can, however, be sure that John carried on the dual role of tailor-parson — his house included a shop, and of his daughters, two if not three were married to tailors, one of them the son of the vicar of Kingston near Lewes.[25]

John Farley wrote his will on 7 January 1599, and left his entire estate to his wife, 'with whom I coupled myself in the fear of God, refusing all other women I linked myself unto her, living with her in the blessed estate of honourable wedlock'.[26] He died in 1601, and the following year his widow settled two copyholds, held of the manor of Keymer, on herself for life, with remainder to her son Henry Farley and his wife Elizabeth; all three were admitted in person on 15 September 1602.[27] Clemence Farley was buried at Keymer on 12 September 1603, and by her will of the previous day, on which she was still capable of making a mark in the form of a key, made her son Henry Farley her executor and residuary legatee.[28] On 7 February 1604 Henry and Elizabeth Farley sold the copyhold property to William Overy, and eighteen months later Henry was in London.[29]

Twenty-eight days before the discovery of the Gunpowder Plot, on 8 October 1605, Henry Farley, scrivener, received the freedom of the City of London, by redemption (that is at his own charge) at the request of Sir Thomas Chaloner, and on 27 March 1606 was admitted to the Scriveners' Company, as the son of John Farley of Keymer in Sussex, tailor, deceased. Most unusually for the period, he had not served an apprenticeship. Henry Farley signs the document in a clear hand and decorates his signature with a flourish, as large as the cramped space allows (fig. 2).[30]

Figure 2.   Henry Farley's signatures, formal and cursive, and a sample of his script, from the Scriveners' Company Common Paper.
Guildhall Library, MS 5370, f. 60r. By kind permission of the Scriveners' Company

Apart from his activities as a promoter of the Cathedral, the next and only official notice of Farley occurs in 1621; on 3 July Henry Farley's former apprentice, Godfrey Austinson, the son of a yeoman from South Milford in Yorkshire, was admitted as a freeman.[31] In the same year John Milton, father of the poet, also released two apprentices. None had after his name the ominous *Artis vero Scriptorie non gnarus* (but ignorant of the art of writing), as did others sworn in the same year. It would seem that only the best apprentices received official approval, and Farley and the elder John Milton turned out three of them.[32]

A definite example of Farley's hand occurs in pen-trials and alphabets written in a slightly juvenile style on several folios of a fourteenth-century manuscript of Bernardus de Gordonio's *Lilium Medicinae* (fig. 3). The identification is secured by

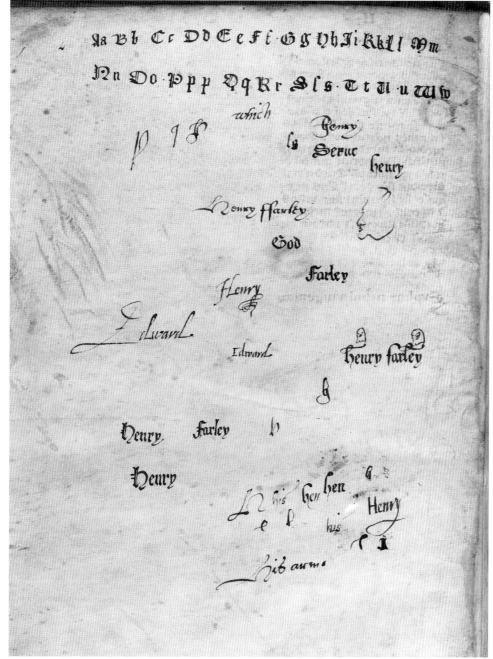

Figure 3.   Henry Farley: a practice alphabet and several signatures.
British Library, Sloane MS 334, f. 301v

two names which link Farley's birthplace with the parish of his upbringing: an ownership-inscription, dating from the middle years of the sixteenth century, of Thomas Duffield, almost certainly to be identified with the Thomas Duffield of East Grinstead, whose will (including unspecified books) was proved in 1579, and the name among the pen-trials of Edward Luxford, doubtless the yeoman of Randolphs in Hurstpierpoint, the parish immediately west of Clayton, who died in 1597. It is tempting to associate the text of a grace, written at the end of the book in an unconfident hand of an earlier generation, as the work of John Farley, the tailor-priest.[33] Henry Farley's hand can also probably be identified in a manuscript copy of Cavendish's *Life of Wolsey*, written in a secretary script of about 1600. The front and back covers are embossed with the name HENRIE FARLEIGH, the letters picked out in gilt.[34]

The records of the Scriveners become erratic after 1628, so we cannot discover from them the date of Farley's death. The author of the article in the *Gentleman's Magazine* of 1780, followed by Nichols in 1828, stated that Farley's zeal 'at last brought him to Ludgate prison', the *at last* implying that he died there.[35] But this assertion is most likely based on Farley's own complaint, published in 1621, that between 1618 and 1620, 'pursued after by Wolves of Wood Street, and the Foxes of the Poultrey ..., instead of serving my Prince ... I was prest for the service of King Lud, where all the comfort I had was that I could see you, salute you, and condole with your miseries: my poore cloathes and ragges I could not compare to anything better than to your West End'. Farley's periphrasis implies a narrow escape from the City compters, or sheriffs' prisons, at Wood Street and Poultry, ending with a term in the debtors' prison at Ludgate, from which the west end of the Cathedral could indeed have been seen.[36]

Neither a will nor administration can be traced for Henry Farley in Sussex or in any of the probate courts having jurisdiction in London.[37] An Elizabeth Farley, perhaps Henry's wife, was buried at Keymer at the beginning of 1621[38] and perhaps Henry, as he had planned to do before hearing of the King's proposed visit to the Cathedral, left for Virginia soon after the appearance of his last publication in 1622.[39]

The Farley name persisted in Sussex: in 1641 a Henry Farley, in the right of his wife Elizabeth, owned Groveland Farm in Cowfold, about seven miles northeast of Clayton; the family remained settled there into the eighteenth century.[40] But there is nothing to connect any of the subsequent Sussex Farleys with the promoter of St Paul's.

HENRY FARLEY'S WRITINGS

The first of Farley's compositions appears to have been the unpublished *Paul's Complaint* presented to the Lord Mayor in 1615; the manuscript is apparently lost. The message having apparently fallen on deaf ears, it was modified for publication as *The Complaint of Paules, to all christian soules* published by Cantrell Legge, one of the printers to Cambridge University, in 1616, the year of our picture (see Appendix 1).[41]

Secondly, Farley wrote a ten-line poem on Queen Anne, accompanied by an engraving by Simon de Passe and dated 1617, found in Henry Holland's *Bazilowlogia* (1618).[42] The Queen died in 1619 and with her all hopes of support from that quarter.

There followed in 1621 *St Paules-Church her bill for the Parliament. As it was presented to the Kings Ma[jes]tie on Midlent-Sunday last* (that is on 26 March 1620), published by Robert Milbourne, a bookseller in St Paul's Churchyard.[43] This pamphlet included the material of a series of intervening attempts to engage the royal attention.

Finally in 1622 Farley brought out *Portland-Stone in Paules-Church-yard. Their birth, their mirth etc*, again published by Milbourne (see Appendix 2).[44]

The Complaint of Paules

The Complaint of Paules, published in 1616, starts with a remarkable frontispiece, laid out to describe the 'ghost' of the silhouette of the spireless Cathedral (figs 4 and 5). The Cathedral speaks in the first person:

THE
COMPLAINT
OF PAVLES,
TO
ALL CHRISTIAN
SOVLES:

OR an humble Supplication,
To our good King and Nation,
For Her newe Reparation.

Written by HENRIE FARLEY.
Amore, Veritate, & Reuerentia.

Printed by CANTRELL LEGGE.
1616.

I Poore *Paules* deiected and diſtreſſed, yet beeing in the beſt proſpect, and taller then all my fellowes) doe ſee, or at leaſt may ſee, (if my windowes be eyes) many ſtately monuments, houſes, and other things builded, and done within theſe fewe yeeres, ſome for Honour, ſome for profit, ſome for Beautie, ſome for pleaſure, ſome for health and recreation, ſome for Royall entertainments and ſports, and many for charitable vſes:

And I haue ſeene the Globe burnt, and quickly made a Phœnix.

Q. But who ſees me? A. Who ſees thee not?

Tunc etiam ſpero,

And hope will ſtill, though ſtill I haue the worſt;
For wer't not for ſome hope, my Heart would burſt.

Figure 4. Title-page of *The Complaint of Paules*, 1616. *British Library*

Figure 5. 'Ghost image' of the Cathedral, shorn of its spire, from *The Complaint. British Library*

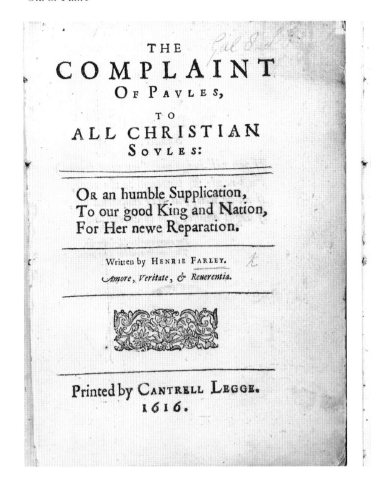

I Poore Paules dejected and distressed, yet beeing in the best prospect, and taller then all my fellowes, doe see, or at least may see, (if my windowes be eyes) many stately monuments, houses, and other things builded, and done within these fewe yeeres, some for Honour, some for profit, some for Beautie, some for pleasure, some for health and recreation, some for Royall entertainments and sports, and many for charitable uses:

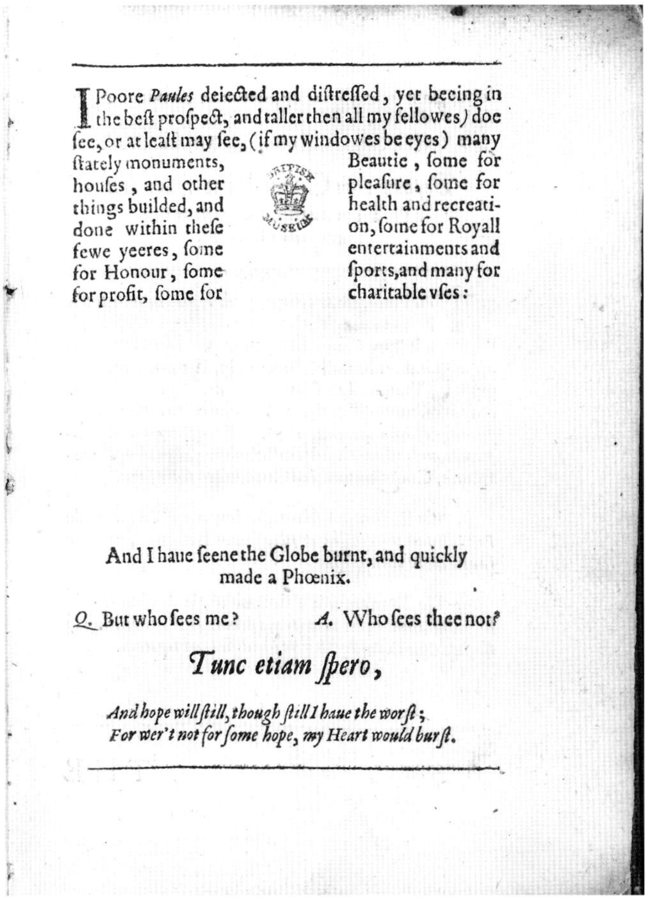

And I have seene the Globe burnt, and quickly made a Phoenix

Q. But who sees me? A. Who sees thee not?
Tunc etiam spero
And hope will still, though still I have the worst;
For wer't not for some hope, my Heart would burst.

After a fanfare of blessings upon the royal household, upon the Bishop ('Their Rev'rend Kingly Father of this *See*')

Blesse this most famous Citie, where I stand
The Flowre, the Perle, the Jemme of Brittaine Land ...

he progresses through the Lord Mayor, officials, citizens, and concludes with:

... the *Noble English hearts*
That in *Virginia* have done *their* parts.

The Cathedral laments its shabby condition, in particular the loss of its spire. There follows the first version of Farley's Dream, set in the context of a sylvan walk leading to a reverie. The actual content of the Dream deals with his vision of the spire restored. The description agrees very largely with the concluding image in our picture (col. pl. III):

My thought the steeple was ta'ne downe,
Lower than the Churches crowne,
And suddenly was rais'd againe,
With good labour not in vaine:
Square it was as t'was before,
Twelve foote higher t'was and more;
Round the top a *battlement*
Seemely faire and excellent,
Above that *battlement* full high
 Four pinacles I did espie
Hollow, and of stone so sure,
That till doomes day would endure:
On the toppe of every one
Was a little spire of stone
At the feete wherof there went,
A little pretty *battlement*:
Round about these *battlements*
Were fine *phanes* and *ornaments*
By whose motion without stay,
Drove the crowes and kites away:
In each *phane* was guilt the *Coate*
Of *benefactors* of best note.

He then enumerates the inhabitants of the angle pinnacles, the King, the Bishop, the Lord Mayor (John Lemon of the Fishmongers' Company was Lord Mayor in 1616) — and lastly a farmer. He goes on to describe pyramids between the pinnacles, giving them also statues, and finally in the centre:

A *curious* and *costly spire* ...
Not too weightie nor too light,
Like *Cheape-cross* it was in sight.

Having peopled this with recently deceased royalty, his eye soared to the apex:

This *spire* was hollow, and with lead
Round about t'was covered ...
In that hollow was nought els,
But a score of little bells,
Which the *Art* of wittie times
Made a delectable chymes.

The dreamer then went out onto the leads and saw the church all mended beneath him. He wanted to go within, but woke up.

While the artist has followed faithfully his architectural instructions, the cast of characters in the various niches departs from the programme (col. pl. III). The largest niche in the spire is occupied now by the King (Farley took every opportunity to display his loyalty to the King). Either side of the new steeple fly four trumpeting angels, each bearing a banner inscribed with a phrase of Farley's devising:

His roiall Seede shall mightie bee and many
And shall increase as much as ere did any.

Like as the Sandes, or Sea, or Starres in Skye,
So shall his people grow and multiply.

This goodlie kinge shall reigne and rule in peace,
Because of him the Gospel doth increase.

He shall be prosperous in all his wayes,
And shall have health, long life and happy dayes.

> He shall have conquestes when he goes to fight,
> And shall put all his enemies to flight.
>
> He shall plant colonies in every nation,
> To forward still the Gospell's propagation.
>
> And at the last to end our blessed story,
> He shall bee crownd in heaven with endless glory.
>
> Where Angels and Archangels ever sings
> All praise and honour to the King of Kings.[45]

Farley spells out his motivation in taking the part of Paul's church: for love of the Church, of his prince and country, and at the bidding of God.

St Paules-Church Her Bill for the Parliament ... 1621

The frontispiece and end-page of this pamphlet are adorned by two versions of the same engraving of a Bishop preaching from Paul's Cross. He is closely surrounded by his audience, but there is no suggestion of a gallery outside the Cathedral, or of the royal party. The view here is taken from the east, and includes to the north a number of houses which must represent Paternoster Row (fig. 6). The print relates to the painting, as it includes the horse led by a groom, the mounting block, and several incidental figures which also appear in the preaching scene picture. In both prints three cartouches fill the space between the preacher and the Cathedral. The texts within these cartouches on the frontispiece, read from top to bottom, are as follows:

a) For the Lord will comfort Zion and repayre all her decayes; Hee will make her Desert like Paradise.
b) And her Wildernesse like the Garden of the Lord. Mirth and joy shall be found there, Thanks

Figure 6. *St Paules-Church her bill for the Parliament*, 1621. Engraving showing Paul's Cross, surrounded by an attentive crowd.
Society of Antiquaries of London

c) giving and the praise of melody. Isaiah 51, 3.

On the back they run:

a) Yea, because of the house of the Lord our
b) God, I will seek to do Thee good. Ps. 122.9
c) [in smaller italics] Blessed may that Preacher bee, That will pray and speake for
    mee. [This verse is surely by Farley]

Farley here returns to his Dream in the very different climate of 1621. By then
the King, perhaps worn down by Farley's appeals, had actually come in procession to St Paul's, and had listened to a sermon preached from Paul's Cross by the
Bishop, John King. It had all happened on Sunday 26 March 1620, and in the text
of this pamphlet Farley explained:

> Here followeth a Petition written in my name, and presented to the King, two dayes
> before his Majestie came to visit me [St Paul's] viz. on Friday the 24th of March 1619
> [1620 new style] But the Master of Requests then attending tooke it away from his
> Highnesse before he could reade it, as many things had been so taken before to the great
> hindrance and griefe of the poor Author.[46]

Farley goes on to give the text of this latest petition, and to follow that by publishing the various appeals he had attempted to give the King between 1616 and
1620:

> done long before, ..., given to the King at sundry times, but not till now published.
> First, ..., the Dream which thou hadst after the Complaint which was *presented by a pic-*
> *ture which you would have given to the King if the petition had not failed* ... [author's italics][47]

It is clear that our diptych took its place as the first of these petitions submitted
between 1616 and 1620. There followed a detailed description of the subject-
matter described in the panels of the picture, expressed as *A dreame in three parts*:

> a scene of 'procession and presents of stone and timber sent by forreigne Princes';
> (col. pl. I).

> the sermon scene: 'the King etc sitting to heare a sermon in the same very place where
> his Majestie did sit indeed when he came to visit you' [St Paul's in 1620] (col. pl. II).

> the Cathedral 'suddenly renewed, beautifully repaired, and cured of all evills and infir-
> mities' accompanied by eight flying angels 'rejoicing with great melody and Sounding
> Praises with Trumpets and heavenly Voices'. (col. pl. III).

Farley then reiterated material from his original manuscript petition of 1615 and
followed that by a Christmas carol written for the King just before he went to
Scotland in 1617, another when the King took a coach at Theobalds on the way,
yet another for presentation at Windsor, and the last on the King's return from
Scotland on Christmas Day 1618.[48]

Farley described the period between his last carol in 1618 and the fulfilment of
his hopes in 1620:

> In this Interim I grew much dismayed, for that I saw little hope of your [St Paul's]
> helpe; many rubs I ranne through, many scoffes and scornes I did undergoe; forsak-
> en by my Butterflie Friends, laught and derided at by your Enemies; pursued after by
> Wolves of Wood Street, and the Foxes of the Poultrey, sometimes Strongly
> Incountred, and sometimes at the point of Death and Despaire: in stead of serving
> my Prince ... I was prest for the service of King Lud, where all the comfort I had was
> that I could see you, salute you, and condole with your miseries: my poore cloathes
> and ragges I could not compare to anything better than to your West End; and my
> service to nothing less than bondage.

Procession to St Paul's from St Mary Overie, as foreseen in 1616. It differs, in the composition of the assembly, the route chosen, and the appearance of the Queen (who would die before the event), from the actual ceremony of 1620. Outer cover of diptych.

Society of Antiquaries of London

Bishop King's sermon before the King from St Paul's Preaching Cross as foreseen in 1616. Again, note the presence of the Queen. The text for the sermon is Farley's suggestion, and not the one used in the event. Left-hand inner panel of diptych.

Society of Antiquaries of London

Henry Farley's vision in 1616 of a rebuilt spire and a restored St Paul's Cathedral. Right-hand inner panel of diptych.

Society of Antiquaries of London

A. James I attended by Queen Anne and Charles, Prince of Wales, going through the final triumphal arch into St Paul's Churchyard. Detail from plate I.
Society of Antiquaries of London

B. Henry Farley on top of the 'mountainous cloud', surveying his vision of the procession. Detail from plate I. *Society of Antiquaries of London*

C. Cheapside: 'This house is to bee lett'. Detail from plate I. *Society of Antiquaries of London*

The banks of the Thames, emphasizing a church with a large tower at the north end of London Bridge, in place of St Magnus Martyr, the Fishmongers' Church, with its modest tower. The Lord Mayor for 1616 was a Fishmonger. Detail of plate I.

Society of Antiquaries of London

A. Shipping, with a very early representation of the Union flag. Detail of plate I.

Society of Antiquaries of London

B. The royal box, with James I, Queen Anne and Prince Charles and aldermen seated below them. Detail of plate II.

Society of Antiquaries of London

The diptych in Gaywood Church, King's Lynn, showing the two Protestant 'deliverances' from the Armada and the Gunpowder Plot. After 1605.

London from Southwark, c. 1630.

Museum of London

The material is here rolled together and printed in 1621 — after the event — but that does not mean that its contents had not been composed in the order Farley claimed. According to the author, all his petitions had fallen on more or less deaf ears. Some had not gone beyond manuscript form until the great procession and sermon of 1620 gave him a modicum of hope of selling copies.

In this essay the Cathedral commands Farley to repeat the details of his vision, and he goes on to give a full account of the three scenes of the diptych, making the point wherever the event differed from its anticipation. As we can see, the picture shows the procession starting at Southwark, winding over London Bridge and along Cheapside. In the *post hoc* pamphlet Farley says that in his Dream the procession — and in this he was mistaken — went from the Tower to St Paul's (the route of the King's royal entry in 1604). In 1620 the procession actually went from Westminster down the Strand, through Temple Bar and up Ludgate Hill.[49]

The artist's version gives as many categories of participants as Farley's Dream but not as numerous or in the same order as the actual procession of 1620, in which the personnel (and they included almost everyone of consequence in the realm) is fully catalogued. Farley had imagined a procession largely composed of clergy and civic dignitaries with a muted group of aristocratic gentlemen and a highly improbable array of fashionable ladies walking behind the Queen. Neither Queen nor ladies would have marched a mile on foot. Moreover the Queen had died before the event and there is no evidence that any ladies took part.

The real procession was a grander event than this painted prophecy of it. It culminated, of course, in the King on horseback, while the painting shows him walking under the last arch on foot at the head of the procession, a most unlikely disposition. Farley's Dream, as here recounted, explains the foreground:

> In this Dream (me thought) I saw presents of stone and timber sent by foreign Princes, to congratulate with his Majestie in that pious work intended for your reparation as Hiram sent to King Solomon.

The geography of the picture telescopes the southern counties to reach the English Channel with ships — one bearing a very early Union Jack (col. pl. VIA). In 1606 the Union Jack, then called the 'Britain flag', was introduced, and could be carried by merchant-men, until a proclamation of 1634 reserved it for men-of-war. An even earlier representation of what looks very like it flew on the Mary Rose.[50] The ships of Farley's Dream are carrying timber and stone, quarried in France. Farley was obviously thinking of Caen stone, the favourite facing material for English Cathedrals throughout the Middle Ages. By the time Farley came to write his last pamphlet, in 1622, *Portland-Stone in Paules-Church-yard* (Appendix 2), there would be no suggestion of imported stone. He gives an informed list of native building stones — Oxford, Ancaster, Beerstone — and exalts the newly acclaimed Portland above all. In 1619 a pier had been built at Portland to ship stone for the Banqueting House at Whitehall; in response to the taste for finely-cut ashlar for Inigo Jones' new classicism, Portland stone had become the favoured material.[51]

There are other discrepancies between the picture and the event. The Queen had died in 1619. The text of the sermon differed from the one Farley had imagined, although the preacher, John King, Bishop of London, was the same. King had been appointed to London in 1611 and was not to die until 1621.

Farley explained the fate of his many petitions:

> Although his Majesties seemed well pleased with anything I gave him in your [St Paul's] behalf, yet I could never get Referency upon any: So that oftentimes I went by *Chearing* Cross in the Morning and home by weeping Cross at night.[52]

In particular, the petition that had accompanied the painting had failed for want of a friend at Court. The friend at Court would have been Sir Thomas Chaloner, but he had died at the end of 1615.

In 1621 Farley puts into the mouth of his Cathedral a fair account of his own plight:

> This poore man ... hath been my voluntary Servant these 8 yeares, by Books, Petitions and other devises, even to his own dilapidations ...[53]

FARLEY'S DREAM

Farley's 'contemplative dreams' ran from 24 July until the end of November 1616. He described the experience thus:

> So dreamed, so wak't, then dream't, then wak'd again,
> As if I had beene made of dreams and sleepe,
> Sometimes I laught, and sometimes waile and weepe,
> By which I called to mind a sacred Theame,
> That all man's life is but a Sleepe or Dreame,
> A Span, a Flower, a Ship at Sea, a Bubble;
> Like to a Tale that's told, like Grasse, like Stubble;
> Like anything that soone doth change and fade,
> Such is the life of man, whom God hath made ...

It has been thought that Farley's Dream was but a literary device to make his appeal more striking. That was probably true of his first reverie of 1615–16, set in a sylvan interlude, represented by the green mountain in the procession panel (col. pl. IVB). That account, however, was immediately followed by the much graver, more sustained episode described in 1621. To read his whole construction as a deliberate fraud is to misunderstand him altogether and greatly underestimate his imaginative powers. Farley had clearly said that the second petition, which accompanied the picture, was turned away at the time. Its content was not printed until 1621. He also said that this second petition depended upon an extended Dream, which he experienced between July and November 1616. This more detailed experience was certainly the basis of the picture, since it included the procession and the preaching, while the first 1616 printed text concentrated on the vision of the rebuilt spire. The assumption that there would not have been time to paint the picture between November 1616 and the end of that year is based on failure to remember that, according to the pre-1752 calendar, 1616 continued until 25 March (1617).[54] It was perfectly possible for this picture to have been painted between November 1616 and the following March.

King James I had launched a Commission to repair St Paul's as early as 1608, the date of Inigo Jones' drawing for a new spire (fig. 7).[55] This is scarcely more realizable than the spire of the diptych which was painted after Jones' return to England in 1615. If there is an association between Jones' 1608 design and the St Paul's diptych, it may have been through Farley's patron Sir Thomas Chaloner. He died on 15 November 1615, but the presence of his initials at the foot of the English and Latin poems *In laudem Authoris* on page 18 of *The Complaint of Paules*, published in 1616 but a reworking of a manuscript of the previous year, demonstrates his involvement with Farley's project. Even without his involvement with Farley, Chaloner, acknowledged as a cultivated man who had been to Italy, would have been interested in the King's Commission for a new feature on St Paul's centre tower — his friend and mentor, Robert Cecil, was one of the Commissioners

Figure 7. Inigo Jones'
design for a new spire for St
Paul's, 1608. Is there also a
suggestion of a dome?
Worcester College, Oxford

who had been instructed to study the Cathedral, its condition and financial
resources in 1608. Thus it could be argued that Farley's vision of 1616 was the
reworking of an idea which had been alive in Cecil's circle, and by extension in
Chaloner's, eight years before.

Farley's cause was reasonable enough, but polite indifference to his pleas gave
them the bitter edge of frustration. In 1621 he put into the mouth of Zeal, looking from one of the western towers, a description of the London streets:

> To see a strange out-landish Fowle,
> A quaint Baboon, an Ape, an Owle,
> A dancing Beare, a Gyant's bone,
> A foolish Ingin move alone,
> A Morris-dance, a Puppit play,
> Mad *Tom* to sing a Roundelay,
> A Woman dancing on a Rope,
> Bull-Baiting also at the *Hope*;
> A Rimer's Jests, a Jugler's cheats,
> A Tumbler shewing cunning feats,
> Or Players acting on the Stage,
> There goes the bounty of our Age.[56]

Farley's 'Dreams' were in themselves quite rational. His persistence may have been the provocation that persuaded James I to set the ball rolling once more in 1620. However, Farley's objective was not seriously attempted until a decade later and not fully realized until the end of the century — and then in circumstances beyond anything that could have been foreseen.

Henry Farley lives in his remarkable writings. His whole body of work, except for the poetic effusion of 1617 in honour of Queen Anne, and that no doubt had the ulterior motive of seeking her patronage, is directed towards the subject of this picture, namely, an appeal for the restoration of the dilapidated St Paul's Cathedral. How could it be that this major church in the heart of the most populous city in England[57] should depend upon the lone voice of a scrivener to stir consciences?

The answer lies in part in St Paul's earlier history. The royal family, of course, owed their allegiance to Westminster Abbey, theatre of their coronations and obsequies. The gentry, although they spent much time at Court, perpetuated their names in the churches attached to their country seats. Dr Caroline Barron has shown how slender were the loyalties of City business men to St Paul's: 'They went there with their heads and with their feet, but their hearts were truly engaged with their parish churches, where they enthusiastically contributed towards their rebuilding and refurbishment, where they founded chantries, joined fraternities and, in the end, chose to be buried ...'.[58] Nor did St Paul's feature as a first choice for the burial of important people in the Tudor and Jacobean periods.[59] None of them established here family mausolea, which might have persuaded their descendants to take care of the Cathedral.

There was still in 1600 a sizeable body of clergy to administer the Cathedral, but while their temporalities had been largely seized by the Crown, there remained the expectation that they were still responsible for the maintenance of the fabric. Dugdale described the predicament of the clergy:[60]

> ... it was acknowledged that the Bishop of London had peculiar care of the whole body of the Church, and the Dean and Chapter of the Quire: but that what each of them enjoyed as to that purpose was so little as that they yearly expended as much upon the roof and other parts decayed, to preserve them from present ruin. Which being made evident to the Commissioners; as also that in former times, even from the very first foundation thereof, it had been supported, partly out of the large oblations of those that visited the shrines and oratories therein; and partly from such public contributions; ... the heat of their enquiry, which, under the pretence of this needful repair, aimed at the ruin of the Bishop, and other members of the church ... began much to cool.

As Dr Barron has shown, John Colet (Dean 1505–19) had made a fleetingly successful bid to improve the popularity of St Paul's by re-organizing the Fraternity of the Holy Name in the Jesus Chapel in the crypt.[61] He had arranged for a bonfire in the churchyard, the chapel had been festooned with greenery and herbs, and bread and ale distributed. The devotion had been popular among Wax Chandlers, Mercers, and under Queen Mary the Stationers. All this, of course, had died with the Reformation.

So in the decade prior to the painting of 'Old St Paul's' and the written appeals that went with it (see Appendices) Henry Farley, earning his living under the shadow of a broken Cathedral, would have found very few sympathizers in his desperate attempt to rescue this stranded ecclesiastical whale.

As William Dugdale said of Farley:

though a private man, he was so zealous to promote the work that he ceased not by sundry petitions to importune the King therein.[62]

So Farley's crusade was still remembered when Dugdale wrote his *History of St Paul's* in 1658.

Is there anything in Farley's biography, insofar as we have been able to reconstruct it, which might explain his devotion to the Cathedral? A series of coincidences link Edmund Grindal, Bishop of London 1559–70, Thomas Chaloner, and the Farley family, and to present them we must return to Sussex in the reign of Queen Mary.

As a teenager, Henry Farley's father might have witnessed the burning of three Protestants in East Grinstead market-place in July 1556, and we may speculate that the event encouraged him on the path which led to his ordination as deacon by Edmund Grindal in 1570. Less than two years into Grindal's episcopate, on 4 June 1561, the great steeple of St Paul's had been struck by lightning, and the resulting fire destroyed a large proportion of the roof.[63] Grindal was tireless in the restoration, and Sir John Hayward, writing half a century later, suggested that Grindal's had been the last work on St Paul's 'worthy of any account', and the chief thing preserving the Bishop's virtuous memory.[64] The baptism of only one child of John and Clemence Farley appears in the East Grinstead registers between 1567 and Henry Farley's christening in 1575, so perhaps John spent time in London preparing for ordination.[65]

One of the benefactors to whom Grindal turned when faced with a Cathedral in ruins was the diplomat and poet Sir Thomas Chaloner, lord of the Bishop's native St Bees in Cumberland; in 1563 Grindal renewed a request to him for six or seven hundred loads of St Bees stone.[66] Sir Thomas was buried in St Paul's in 1565, with Burghley as his chief mourner, leaving an only son, the second Thomas (1561–1615), only four years old. At the behest of Burghley, the boy was educated at St Paul's School and Magdalen College, Oxford. He grew to be the epitome of *The Compleat Gentleman*. Henry Peacham would describe him as:

the truly honest, and sometime lover of all excellent parts, Sir Thomas Chaloner.[67]

Chaloner's education under the shadow of St Paul's Cathedral, where his father lay entombed, suggests a close acquaintance with the building. One of the pieces in the elder Chaloner's collection of Latin poems, posthumously published in 1579 when his son had reached the impressionable age of eighteen, was a lament for St Paul's, originally published in 1561, the year of the lightning-strike.[68]

> Till by a sad Mischance
>   this stately Pile,
> Which stood so long
>   the Glory of our Isle;
> And (as the Sun the
>   Moon and Stars outvies
> The Beauty and the
>   Lustre of the Skies)
> Did through the Clouds
>   Soar with its lofty Top
> The Heavens, like Atlas
>   to uphold and prop;
> Is now brought lower,
>   and its towring Spire

Level'd, and burnt by
  Lightnings rapid Fire, etc.

Henceforth compute,
  That nothing stable is
But flows away,
  decays, and vanishes.
Since this strong Fabrick,
  hard as any Rock
Which near a Thousand
  Years had borne the shock
Of Storms and Tempests,
  with the rude assaults
Of boisterous Gales,
  burst from Eolian Vaults,
Torrents of Rain,
  Vollies of Hail and Snow,
Enough to make the
  World's Foundation bow;
Hurricanes, Whirlwinds,
  and the Batteries
Of all the loud Artillery
  Of the Skies.

The Summers and the
  Winters rough Attacks,
With all their Times and
  Years upon its Back,
Could bear no longer;
  but to Fate at last
Submit its self, and falls
  by Lightnings Blast.
The Steeple, Roof, and
  all PAULS former height,
Sank down and henceforth
  vanish'd out of sight.
Hard, cruel Fate! that
  everything should be
A Prey to
  ravenous Mortality.

The younger Sir Thomas escorted King James and his family to England in 1603, and later became manager of Queen Anne's private estates; the fortunes of this distinguished courtier, traveller, linguist, philosopher and botanist were locked into those of the Cecils and the new dynasty. More significant to our story is that it was the same Thomas Chaloner who sponsored Henry Farley's freedom of the City of London in 1605, and whose initials appear below the encomium *In laudem Authoris* in Farley's *The Complaint of Paules*.

JOHN GIPKYN, *FLORUIT* 1594–1629

John Gipkyn was the artist Farley employed to paint this picture. Gipkyn's forefather was John Gepeking of St Paul's Churchyard, a book-craft artist recorded in the Return of Aliens for 1541. He was admitted without payment as a founder-member of the Stationers' Company, which in 1554 moved to St Peter's College on the south side of St Paul's Churchyard.[69] Two books published in 1551 show the imprimatur of John 'Gykim' or 'Gybkyn', and his address is given on the title page as 'Pauls Churchyard at the Spread Eagle'[70] on Franciscus Perussellus' *Summa Christianae Religionis*. Gipkyn senior was mentioned again in the Stationers' records for 1586.[71] At that time his son, another John Gipkyn, was admitted a freeman of the Stationers' Company but not sworn *quia surdus et mutus est* (because he is deaf and dumb). Despite his disabilities this John Gipkyn immediately set about acquiring an apprentice and on 30 September 1594 the third generation of John Gipkyns was registered as an apprentice to his father, the deaf John Gipkyn.[72]

Of the career of this third John Gipkyn, painter, we know a good deal, and there is a strong presumption that the young Stationer changed companies to become an artist and artistic entrepreneur; he can be traced as such between 1604 and 1629. At the top end of his market, so to speak, his self-portrait was listed in Vertue's inventory of Charles II's *Alphabet of Painters Names, mentioned in the King's Catalogue of Pictures, 1687 whose works were then in the Royal Collection, in the palaces of Windsor, Whitehall, St James's etc. Every one of these painters had been employed, at times by several of the Kings, Queens and Princes etc.*[73] It would be interesting to know what royal employment Gipkyn had undertaken; it was probably in relation to a masque at Court.

Gipkyn and Lord William Howard of Naworth

Gipkyn was employed by Lord William Howard of Naworth (1563–1640), uncle of the great patron of the arts, Thomas Howard, second Earl of Arundel who was a friend of Inigo Jones. William Howard was a founder-member of the original Elizabethan Society of Antiquaries and a friend of Sir Robert Cotton. Gipkyn may well have worked for Howard before October 1619 when he was paid 26 shillings. for a picture of the family hero, the Earl of Arundel. This picture of Earl Phillip, William's half-brother, who had died in the Tower in 1595, is a copy of the one now at Castle Howard. Also in 1619 'Grinkin' was paid 'for drawing things for Mount Pleasant, 6 shillings, and for a lodestone [a magnet] 5 shillings'. In May 1620 he was paid for 'sundry cullers' 7s., and in the same year for 'drawing a plat for my Lord 6 shillings'. In 1621 he mended 'the lodestone and my Lord's watch'.[74]

Gipkyn and the Pageants

Gipkyn's staple employ, however, was for some of the most extravagant ephemera of his time. In 1604, 1609, 1610, 1611, 1613, and 1618 he was the artist for the Lord Mayor's shows.[75] In 1604 he collaborated with Ben Jonson, working for the Haberdashers' Company, for which he supplied a chariot and a lion, two galleys, fireworks, banners, etc. The 1609 pageant for the Ironmongers boasted a flying dragon, a unicorn, an ocean with mermaids and tritons, a whale with a blackamoor in his mouth, making music and casting water from his mouth and fire from his fins. In 1610, for the Merchant Taylors, Gipkyn painted a ship, three lions, two unicorns, a camel and two giants, and a special pageant of Merlin in the Rock.[76] On other occasions Gipkyn collaborated with Anthony Munday and with the playwright Thomas Middleton. There is one precious survival: the original coloured drawing for the Fishmongers' pageant, *Chrysalanalia: the Golden Fishing*, for which Munday wrote the text (fig. 8).[77] Gipkyn's last pageant with

Figure 8.   Design for *Chrysalanalia: the Golden Fishing*, 1616, the pageant for the Lord Mayor,
John Lemon, written by Anthony Munday and devised by Mr Clay and Mr Kemby. The diptych, painted in the same year, gives special prominence to St Magnus, the Fishmongers'
church, as a compliment to the Lord Mayor.
Society of Antiquaries of London

Munday was in 1618 for the Ironmongers' Company when the day was chosen
to coincide with the execution of Sir Walter Raleigh, in the hope of drawing the
crowds away from Old Palace Yard at Westminster. That is some gauge of the
popularity of these pageants, which tended to cost about the same amount as
their courtly counterparts, the royal masques, that is about £750 each. The
records give some idea of the resources demanded on these occasions, which
reached their apogee during the years Gipkyn was working on them.[78] Gipkyn's
pageant for the Ironmongers in 1618 was his last; thereafter he was superseded
by Gerard Christmas, working with Thomas Middleton or Thomas Dekker.

In all the pageant accounts of the City livery companies, Gipkyn is described
not as a stationer but as a painter-stainer. His career begins before the surviving
lists of members of the Painter-Stainers' Company, but the court minutes of the
Company for 1623–49 exist, and here not just one but two 'Gypkyns' appear.[79]
It is evident from the pattern of John Gipkyn's commissions that he must have
had assistants, one of whom may have been a relative. A Samuel Gypkin was
ordered to pay his debts in April 1629. On the same page is an entry for 8
October:

> John Gybkin, an ancient brother of this company, paid at this court 6 shillings of his
> old debt, requesting the company to remit the rest; but this court doth think it fitt that
> he shall stand to pay the rest when he shall be abell.

That is the last we hear of John Gipkyn. Despite the patronage of Lord William
Howard he had not been able to stave off the ruin brought about by the successful bid of Gerard Christmas to take over the Lord Mayor's pageants, and his
end may have been sad.

Gipkyn and the theatre

In 1618 and 1620 Gipkyn worked for another private patron, whose involvement brings us very close to the theatre. His collaborator in the pageants had been Anthony Munday, who also wrote plays for the Admiral's Men, a company in which Edward Alleyn took the lead from 1593 to 1604.[80] In his retirement from active performance Alleyn founded the College of God's Gift in Dulwich (1613) and for the edification of its students he commissioned a series of paintings of English Kings.[81] On 29 September 1618 he ordered bust-length portraits, starting with the four Tudor monarchs — Henry VIII, Edward VI, Mary and Elizabeth — plus the reigning James I, and Henry V as the greatest role-model. They are recognizable, if very bad, copies of the standard painted portrait types. Nine days later he extended the series back to Edward III, that is he added the Plantagenets, of whom there were likewise known portrait types.[82] In September 1620 he ordered another batch of earlier Kings, also the Black Prince and Anne Boleyn. In November Alleyn added a set of twelve Sibyls, this time mentioning the artist, 'Mr Gipkyn'. It seems probable that Gipkyn painted, or at least supplied, both Kings and Sibyls.

Gipkyn supplied Edward Alleyn with another extensive cycle, this time of Christ and His Mother and the twelve Apostles.[83] These have not survived. As a true Protestant, Alleyn also included a series of five Reformers including Calvin and Luther. A singleton of Dante may suggest there was a run of Poets as well.[84]

None of these pictures is above the level of hack work, and if they all came from Gipkyn, they may have been partly from the brush of Samuel Gipkyn rather than John. They were very cheap; when Alleyn wanted something special he went to Rowland Buckett who was one of the Masters of the Painter-Stainers' Company to sit in judgement on the two Gipkyns and their debts in 1629.[85]

On 13 September 1619 the deed and the statutes of Dulwich College were read in the College Chapel in the presence of men who had helped Alleyn to obtain his charter: Francis Bacon, then Lord Chancellor, Thomas Howard, Earl of Arundel (nephew of Gipkyn's patron), Henry Howard, and Inigo Jones. Why was Inigo Jones there? There was one context in which Alleyn could have forged a strong association with Inigo Jones: through the theatre. Furthermore, Alleyn's library included a copy of Farley's first pamphlet, *The Complaint of Paules*.[86]

Edward Alleyn's last theatrical appearance had been as the personification of the Genius of the City in the triumphal arch of *Londinium*, the first of the series of arches through which James I's coronation procession had been intended to wind its way (fig. 9). On account of the plague, however, the public part of the ceremonial was delayed until 15 March 1604. A record of this ambitious Triumph was published in the same year.[87] The arch in Fenchurch Street signifying *Londinium* was arrayed with largely mute figures, portraying Brittayne Majesty, Divine Wisdom, Father Thames reclining at the bottom with real fish sporting in his bowl, and the Genius of London, played by Edward Alleyn, with a speaking part written by Ben Jonson. Alleyn was:

> attired, rich, reverend and antique, hair long and white crowned with a wreath of a plane tree, mantle and buskins purple ... His speech was delivered with excellent action and a well-tuned audible voice:

> ... Now London rear
> Thy forehead high, and on it strive to wear
> Thy choicest gems: teach thy steep towers to rise

Figure 9. Stephen Harrison's first arch, *Londinium*, from his *Arches of Triumph erected in Honour of James I*, 1604. The arch is crowned with a prospect of London's waterfront from St Bride's Church to Fishmongers' Hall. St Paul's Cathedral crowns the City and St Magnus is emphasized. *Society of Antiquaries of London*

> Higher with people, set with sparkling eyes
> Thy spacious windows; and in every street
> Let thronging Joy, Love and Amazement meet.

Harrison, and Nichols following him, described the arch before which Alleyn delivered his speech:

> The upper roofe therof ... bore up the true moddells of all the notable houses, turrets and steeples within the Citie.

In other words, this is a capriccio of the most famous features of London, the kind of thing associated with Panini and the Grand Tour, but in fact a device with roots in classical wall-paintings. As such this panorama is justly famous among students of the topography of London. After the Cathedral itself, the most striking building in the composition is a very large square tower with four mighty

Figure 10.   Detail from John
Norden's *Panorama of London*,
1600, showing the artist working
from the top of the tower of St
Mary Overie.
Guildhall Library

angle pinnacles. If you look carefully at Gipkyn's prospect of London from
Southwark, you will discover the same feature immediately north of London
Bridge on its east side (col. pl. V). That is the position occupied by St Magnus
Martyr, the church of the Fishmongers' Company. The prominence of this
church and the emblems on the imagined central confection for the Cathedral is
a compliment to the Fishmongers whose Master was Lord Mayor in the year the
picture was painted. We know the squat western tower of St Magnus Martyr, with
one turret for the staircase, from numerous views, notably the Copperplate of
c. 1553. Gipkyn's tower resembles no London tower of the pre-Fire period as
much as it resembles the object on top of *Londinium*.

Even though Gipkyn knew and worked all his life under the shadow of St
Paul's, he turned to prints, even old prints, rather than to first-hand experience
for his record of the City. For the church towers, for Bow, the Royal Exchange,
the Dutch church, for the Guildhall, and for most of the identifiable buildings in
his view of London, he looked no further than Norden's panorama of 1600.[88]
Norden actually engraved into his view a little figure of himself levelling up the
prospect for this prodigious work; he was standing, of course, on the roof of St
Mary Overie (fig. 10). A visit to that same roof today confirms that the surviving landmarks are indeed aligned as he drew them.

In publishing the painted view of London of *c.* 1630 taken from the same vantage-point, the Museum of London dismissed Gipkyn's effort of fourteen years
before as of no topographical value.[89] Does not the Museum of London's painting (col. pl. VIII) also depend upon Norden, or upon Visscher, who in 1616
copied Norden? (fig. 11).

Artists such as Claude de Jonghe, fine though their studies of lesser groups of
buildings might be, also turned to prints when it came to the daunting task of a
prospect of London. As Maurice Howard has pointed out, 'a long tradition,
largely at the hands of Flemish artists links the Wyngaerde panorama of London
of the mid-sixteenth century to the paintings of the City by such artists as Claude
de Jonghe in the 1630s'.[90]

Gipkyn had other messages to convey as well as the topographical one. The
improbable mountain behind his impossible version of the Tower of London
is a case in point (col. pl. IVB). It may be said to represent Farley's Virgilian
reverie that prompted the first version of his Dream. If so, it does so in rather
a perverse way. Farley made it clear in that first description that he mused by
the bank of a stream, in the way honoured in contemporary images of the
meditative man.

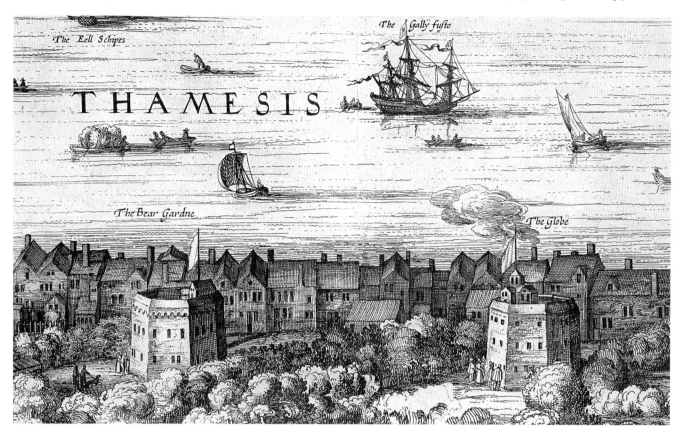

Figure 11.   Detail from
Nicholas Visscher's panorama
of London, *c.* 1616, showing
the Globe Theatre and the
Bear Garden. No churches are
visible.
Guildhall Library

In Gipkyn's picture, however, the stream has been metamorphosed into the
top of a mountain or cloud. Here Gipkyn's wide experience of City pageantry
stood him in good stead. His pageant for 1613 had taken the theme of *The
Triumph of Truth*.[91] The various protagonists assembled in Paul's Churchyard, and
pointed towards a Mount Triumphant close by Little Conduit. This Mount is:

> overspredde with a thick sulphorous darknesse, being a fog or miste raised from
> Error, enviously to blemish that place which bears the title of London's Mount
> Triumphant — the chief grace and lustre of the whole Triumph.

Truth laments:

> Thick are the mists that o're faire Cities rise;
> I know there stands no other envious bar
> But that foule cloude to darken this bright day,
> Which with this fanne of starres I'll chace away,
> Vanish suspicious fog! that I may see
> This Cities grace, that takes her light from mee.

Whereupon the cloud rises and the Mount appears in glory. The four monsters
— Barbarism, Ignorance, Impudence, and Falsehood — whose job it had been
to control the 'cloud', fall flat, and reveal London enthroned, with above her
Religion flanked by Liberality and Perfect Love. As the pageant progressed, the
veiling and unveiling was repeated.

What would have been difficult to achieve on the street was easier to suggest
in paint and we may hazard that the mountainous cloud overshadowing the east
end of Gipkyn's panorama (col. pl. IVB), with the suggestion of gleaming buildings half way up, and Farley leaning over the top to survey the whole, represents

the 'thick sulphorous darkness' overshadowing Mount Triumphant as described in the pageant, *The Triumph of Truth* (1613), for which Thomas Middleton provided the programme and John Gipkyn the contrivances.

THE ROLE OF THOMAS MIDDLETON, PLAYWRIGHT

There can be no doubt that Thomas Middleton and Edward Alleyn both knew and used the services of John Gipkyn. I suggest that the feature of a holy mountain or cloud looming over the cityscape on the outer panel of Gipkyn's painting refers to the Mount Triumphant and the cloud of sulphurous darkness which at times covered it and at times was withdrawn, derived from Middleton's pageant, *The Triumph of Truth*. Not only was Gipkyn responsible for 'realizing' this fantasy on a moving stage, but it is also likely that Henry Farley witnessed or heard about the pageant. It would have been difficult to avoid.

Two more details in Gipkyn's painting confirm his working relationship with Middleton. In the preaching scene there is a group of twelve choir boys assembled on the roof of the gallery (col. pl. VIB). The deployment of singers to give voice from high places was a tradition followed in major churches.[92] The tradition has been revived for the Palm Sunday procession at Salisbury and the custom is still honoured on May-day on the roof of the tower of Magdalen College, Oxford. Its popularity in a secular context in Elizabethan London was described by Louis Grenade:

> Around the tower of the [Royal] Exchange are two galleries, one above the other, very well built, where the musicians of the City perform marvels of sound on Sundays at 4 o'clock in the afternoon, when the days are long, to the great contentment of they who hear, and their number is very large.[93]

The Children of Paul's (a company of boy actors recruited from the Cathedral choristers) were exceedingly busy outside canonical hours, for they performed plays written for them by George Chapman, Ben Jonson, John Marston and Thomas Middleton. It appears they stopped performing in 1606, but for the previous decade they had been working in private theatres and in the great cloister at St Paul's, which was to the west of the north transept. Middleton wrote for them *A Trick to Catch the Old-One* (written 1604–7, published 1608) and *A Chaste Mayd in Cheap-side* (written 1613, published 1630) in the same mould of a citizen comedy. The action takes place on the ground floor of a property in Cheapside (which would have been partly a shop) belonging to a prosperous goldsmith.[94] The property falls into the hands of Mr and Mrs Allwit. They rejoice:

Allwit:	What shall we do now wife?
Mistress Allwit:	As we were wont to do.
Allwit:	We are richly furnish'd, wife, with household stuff.
Mistress Allwit:	Let's let out lodgings then
	And take a house in the Strand.
Allwit:	In truth, a match, wench:
	We are simply stock'd with cloth-of-tissue cushions,
	To furnish out bay-windows; push, what not that's quaint
	And costly, from the top to the bottom.
	Life, for furniture, we may lodge a countess![95]

The response of the Allwits to coming into possession of the house and contents is to 'let out lodgings then, And take a house in the Strand'. The second decade of the seventeenth century saw a general drift of wealth westward from

Cheapside along the main artery towards the Strand and the magnet of the court at Whitehall. This is reflected in Gipkyn's painting: one of the most splendid façades behind the procession along Cheapside has an inscription scrawled across it, 'This house is to bee lett' (col. pl. IVC).

Gipkyn's Work for Henry Farley

While work for Thomas Middleton was no doubt very demanding it would not have been so puzzling as working for the elusive, single-minded hermit, Henry Farley. Gipkyn could draw on his recent experience of a mountain with a dark gauze over it to suggest Farley's vantage-point for his vision, but there remained the problem of reconciling the 'High Place', from which Farley surveys the scene, and the secluded brook where he claims to have first entertained his Dream. That reconciliation is a literary one, and comes from another book, after *The Bible*, *The Book of Common Prayer* and Foxe's *Book of Martyrs*, that might have been found at the Farley home in Keymer: *Piers Plowman*.

That poem begins with just such a pastoral walk and rest beside the stream that Farley described in his first version, then moves to the 'ferly' or vision where he finds himself in a wilderness with a wide panorama before him. This passage explains much in the painting: even the mysterious square tower, the pastoral interlude with a shepherd and sheep below him, as well as the glimpse of a golden city half-way down the mountain with fragments of an inscription across it.[96]

> But on a May morning, on Malvern Hills,
> There befell me a ferly, of fairy methought.
> I was wearily wandered out, and went me to rest
> Under a broad bank by a brook's side,
> And as I lay and leaned, and looked into the waters,
> I slumbered into sleep, it sounded so merry.
> Then did I meet a marvellous sweven,
> That I was in a wilderness wist I never where;
> As I looked into the east, high into the sun,
> I saw a tower on a toft, triely made;
> A deep dale beneath, a dungeon therein
> With deep ditches and dark and dreadful to see.
> A fair field full of folk found I there between,
> Of all manner of men, the mean and the rich,
> Working and wandering as the world demands.[97]

Several other well-known features of London have been modified in Gipkyn's painting. The array of heads on poles, so conspicuous a greeting to the visitor reaching London Bridge from the south, has been left out; they would have been a jarring element in this vista of New Troy (col. pl. V). Other important buildings on the Bridge have been omitted because they would have obscured the view of the procession. This has been contrived to begin at the most important religious site on the south bank of the Thames, St Mary Overie.

Something has been added, however, showing how carefully this picture was programmed. If Norden, Gipkyn or Farley had turned to the west from their vantage point on the central tower of St Mary Overie, they would have seen, beyond the Bishop of Winchester's town house, which Gipkyn includes (and of which a gable wall still exists) the Clink, the Bear Pit and the Bull Baiting arena (fig. 11). Beyond lay the theatres, the Rose and the Globe, but we find no trace of any of them in the painting. In Gipkyn's panorama, instead of the places of

entertainment, we find at least four churches, one with an octagonal turret above a square base. There were, in fact, no churches along the south bank to the west of Southwark — Gipkyn had been instructed to transform London's 'red-light' district into a place of piety. Gipkyn's prospect of London is in the tradition of the medieval views of cities. Like his ancestors before him he felt at liberty to sacrifice topography, including telescoping England south of London, in the interests of the message. For the necessary sprinkling of recognizable features, he turned to engravings, as he had done in supplying portraits of the great for Edward Alleyn, and in contriving angels to flutter round the restored glories of a rejuvenated St Paul's.[98]

When it came to describing the north-east angle of the Cathedral itself, which he probably walked past five times a week, Gipkyn added nothing to what we know from earlier prints. Penrose's archaeological investigations show us that his placing of Paul's Cross in relationship to the much longer eastern arm is correct.[99] But Gipkyn offers us an array of windows which bear little relation to reality. Better to believe Hollar's drawing of 1647 published by Dugdale (fig. 12), where the eastern arm on the northern side of the Cathedral had not been refaced by Inigo Jones. Gipkyn probably derived the view of this angle of the Cathedral from a corner of the map of Britain in John Speed's *Theatre of Great Britain*, 1611 (fig. 13).

Gipkyn seems to have been more interested in the gallery for listening to sermons at the Cross (col. pl. VIB).[100] The provision of shelter for the audience was originally contrived by means of an awning, superseded by a permanent gallery which was in place by 1483 (both outdoor pulpit and gallery were cleared away in 1643 by Oliver Cromwell). There is another version of the preaching scene, a small print embellishing the title-page at the end of Farley's second publication, *St Paules-*

Figure 12.   St Paul's from the north by Wenceslaus Hollar, drawn 1647, published by Dugdale, 1658. Note the convincing rendering of surviving medieval fenestration in the north choir aisle.
Society of Antiquaries of London

Figure 13. Vignette from
John Speed's *Theatre of Great
Britain*, 1611, showing St Paul's
from approximately the same
angle as the preaching scene,
and with similar, fictional windows. Note the preaching
cross.
Society of Antiquaries of London

Church her bill for the Parliament (1621) (fig. 6). The omission of the royal box suggests the print may have been intended for more general purposes.[101]

Farley has insisted on pointing out the iniquity of houses tucked into the east
wall of the north transept, as they certainly were (col. pl. II). His pamphlet of
1621 provides the text for all but one of the inscriptions and one of them refers
to the houses abutting the Cathedral:

See O King how my wall creepers have made me work for chimney sweepers.

The removal of these intrusive houses was one of the first acts of the post-1620 initiative to restore the Cathedral. It caused much distress, as the tenants were not properly compensated for the loss of their homes.[102] The chimneys of these houses were no doubt a contributory factor, but the grimy condition of the exterior of the Cathedral was a symptom of a more widespread problem. Perhaps Gipkyn's and Middleton's 'sulphorous darknesse, being a fog or miste raised from Error' had a more than metaphorical reality. Not only was Old St Paul's coated in grime, its successor would be black before it was finished. The fog of atmospheric pollution had begun.

Gipkyn had a poor grasp of architectural perspective. He offered a view of the east end of the Cathedral with its famous rose window in which two facets of the central tower are flattened out. That tower was composed on each face of three very high lancets surmounted by a blind gallery and above that a further lower group of another three lancets. The weight of the original spire was supported by an elegant series of flying buttresses which came down not, as he suggests, onto the roof, but onto the re-entrant angles of the transepts. It is plain Gipkyn could not bring his pencil to depict a Gothic arch, so all arches are rounded.

The panel featuring the sermon at Paul's Cross shows a couple in the foreground, talking. Two horses are clopping away. A dog is barking furiously and a whipper is making matters worse by beating it. The group of choir boys stationed on the roof of the gallery must have ushered in the sermon with a hymn. People are going in and out through the north transept to contribute to the alms boxes. The final touch is that we have the text of the sermon that is being preached which confirms the opinion of Sir Francis Nethersole that the purpose of the event was to promote the rebuilding of St Paul's. Nethersole wrote to Sir Dudley Carleton five days before the King's visit

> The Catholics say that the King's approaching visit to St Paul's is to hear the Bishop of London preach on the Spanish match; the Protestants that he goes to exhort the people to contribute for the King of Bohemia, who will be publicly prayed for; the truth being that it is to advance the contributions towards the rebuilding of St Paul's.[103]

All this was in contrast to the Babel within. Farley had pithy comments on the abuse of the interior, described by John Earle in his *Micro-Cosmographie* of 1628:[104]

> It is a heape of stones and men, with a vast confusion of Languages ... The noise in it is like that of Bees, a strange humming or buzze-mixt of walking, tongues and feet: It is a kind of still roare or loud whisper. It is the great Exchange of all discourse ... and they are not half so busie at the Parliament.

So the royal visit and setting-in-hand of repairs did nothing to change the scandal of the nave as it had been since Elizabeth's reign. Dugdale quoted *The Gul's Horn Book* of 1609 where there is a chapter on the various abuses:

> The *South Alley* for Usury and Popery the *North for Simony* and the Horse faire in the middest for all kinds of bargains, meetings, brawlings, murthers, conspiracies, and the *Font* for ordinary Paimentes of money, are so well known to all men as the beggar knows his dish.[105]

When we come at last to Farley's vision of the restored St Paul's (col. pl. III), it has to be acknowledged that his termination for the tower is quite unintelligible, since he shows two angles flattened out. Neither Farley nor Gipkyn had any architectural training. Farley might have had a privileged glimpse, or at least a verbal description, of Inigo Jones' 1608 design. Jones' general concept is comparable, but Farley's version is a flimsy framework for royalist propaganda, with the royal family occupying niches up the spire and its supporting pinnacles, with further inscriptions on panels:

> Blessed be the peace makers.

> Touch not the Lord's Anointed,
> nor do his prophets any harm.

The Glory at the top of both the procession and the transformed St Paul's scenes was probably taken from the engraved title page by Cornelius Boel for the 1611 King James Bible. It was a common motif at the time.

On the procession panel, over the entrance to the churchyard Gipkyn had been required to inscribe:

> Behold the King cometh with great joy.

Two further inscriptions radiate upon the procession scene from the Glory at the apex:

> For thy temple's sake I wish thee all prosperity.

> Many good things are donne in thee, O thou fayre citie.

Farley left no stone unturned to convey his meaning. The only literary mistake he made was in the choice of text for the actual sermon. At the base of the preaching scene he introduced a latecomer who asks one of the audience:

> I pray, Sir, what is the text?

to which the elderly gentleman replies in mirror-writing:

> The second of Chronicles, chapter xxiv.

As we shall see, King James gave his Bishop a different text.

Against Gipkyn's limitations must be set an admiration for the range of his talents — from a lodestone to a Cathedral, from a whale spouting fire and water to portraits of Kings, Sibyls, Apostles, Poets and Protestants. He was a Renaissance man indeed, and if he turned to engravings to help him out at every available turn, who can blame him? The demands made on artists in Catholic countries after the Reformation were to infuse the subjects of the faith with a new passion; in Protestant countries to tackle entirely new visual territory.

This picture belongs to a category of paintings more notable for the problems they pose than for their beauty. Those problems are well worth teasing out, for they offer insights into the minds of several generations of British people for whom the scheme of eternal verities had been overturned and overturned again. With the Reformation, the familiar landmarks of Christianity and Christian art became taboo overnight. Long treasured and revered images were destroyed wholesale. A universally understood religious language fell silent. The rise of portraiture, which plays a part in this painting, could not satisfy those used to believing in something more important than themselves. Even the deliberate attempt to invest portraits of the sovereign with something more than human dignity could not fill the gap. The vacuum is circumscribed, if not filled, by the curious group of programmed pictures of which this diptych is one.

The most important thing these pictures have in common is that they were evidently devised by someone other than the painter, someone who worked out what they wanted in some detail, and often supplied texts to explain the imagery. One class of such images is a set of scurrilous anti-Catholic pictures, of which 'The Four Evangelists stoning the Pope' painted for Henry VIII, now at Hampton Court, is an example. Less offensive, but scarcely less politically slanted, is the series of history paintings of events in the reign of Henry VIII, and group images of his family, also at Hampton Court.

The triptych (three-leaf) and the diptych (two-leaf) forms for a picture, both of which had been commonly used for altarpieces, are as old as their Greek-derived names suggest, and stem from hinged wax or ivory inscribed tablets of classical antiquity. The triptych, which may fold to the centre during Lent, revealing more sober subject-matter on the exterior of the wings, was peculiarly well adapted for high altars. The diptych, on the other hand, follows the formula of a book, and is particularly suitable for private devotional images. Medieval diptychs were small, intimate objects, intended for quiet prayer at a prie-dieu, the pre-eminent example in England being the Wilton Diptych. Among post-medieval adaptations of the diptych form, the painting that most closely resembles the 'Old St Paul's' diptych is another on a similar scale showing Queen Elizabeth at Tilbury and the discovery of the Gunpowder Plot (col. pl. VII). This was presented to Gaywood church, King's Lynn, by the Revd Thomas Hares, the rector there between 1598 and 1634, who was probably its original owner.[106] Both diptychs illustrate sermons and it is not beyond possibility that the Gaywood diptych was also painted by John Gipkyn.

Both works combine quasi-historical images of royal activity with obvious morals; both enlist inscriptions to elucidate novel iconography and point the message; both incorporate recognizable figures of the monarchs. They differ in that the Gaywood picture is clearly retrospective and congratulatory: the delivery of England from the Spanish Armada in 1588 and from a 'Popish Plot' in 1605, were interpreted at the time as the divine ratification of Protestantism, an equivalent of the crossing of the Red Sea. The 'Old St Paul's' painting, on the other hand, purports to be, and I believe was, prophetic.

THE SERMON OF JOHN KING, BISHOP OF LONDON, 1620

The sermon at Paul's Cross required full orchestration, and Bishop King rose to the occasion (fig. 14). His sermon is about 10,000 words long and would have taken at least an hour and a half to deliver. King James had given the Bishop the text:

> Thou shalt arise and have mercy upon Sion, for the time to favour hir, yea the set time is come. For thy servants take pleasure in hir stones, and favour the dust thereof ... (Psalm 102, verses 13–14)

The Bishop opened by discerning two rivers of mercy, one from God, the other from man, meeting in Sion. He described mercy as a cloud of rain in a time of drought. He goes on to speak of St Paul's Cathedral as possessing a

> Sickly and crazie constitution, sick of age in it selfe and with many aches in her joints ... raised out of the ashes of a fire 1,000 years ago as a phoenix, to be touched with a coal from the altar of God 500 years later which consumed the crest and vertical point.

He contrasts the plight of St Paul's with the glory of London:

Figure 14.   Portrait of John
King, Bishop of London from
1611 until his death in 1621.
Painted by Nicholas Lockey
and engraved by Simon de
Passe.
St Paul's Cathedral: Sampson Lloyd

England the ring of Europe, your City the gemme. If England the body, the City the
eye, your Cathedral the apple of it ... Here the Chamber of our British Empire ... that
forest of Masts on your river ... that more than miraculous Bridge ... your Royal
Exchange for Merchants, your Halls for Companies, your Gates for Defence, your
Markets for Victuals, your Aqueducts for Water, your Granaries for Provision, your
Hospitalls for the Poor, your Bridewells for the Idle, your Chamber for Orphans, and
your Churches for Holy Assemblies (and I hope the cleaning of the River will follow)

— your English Colonie in Virginia ... hath drawn from the breast of this Citty and Diocese a £1000 towards hir church.

He winds down to the necessity of pouring money into the upkeep of St Paul's, with a peroration on the glory of giving.

John King (1559?-1621) stands among the masters of the golden age of English spiritual writing, alongside Lancelot Andrewes and John Donne. A collection of fifty-two of his sermons upon the book of Jonas, given at York in 1594, was printed in 1597, to be sold in St Paul's Churchyard.[107] A recurrent theme of these sermons was the Resurrection:

> Even so we shall rise again ... our night wherein we sleep awhile shall be changed into a morning, and after obscurity in the pit of forgetfulness, we shall appear and shine as the stars of God in their happiest Season ... our Phoenix rose from his ashes, the first born of the dead was born from the wombe of earth.

In so speaking, the Bishop mentioned that elsewhere he had proved the Resurrection. That claim, and the text of it (not yet discovered), accounts for the word which Bishop King gave to St Paul's, and which shines today as the true core of this great place. 'Even so,' he wrote, 'we shall arise again.' This declaration is the next step beyond *Resurrexit sicut dixit*, After three days *I* will rise again — *Resurgam*.

We are familiar with the tale told in *Parentalia* of Sir Christopher Wren laying out the foundations of the new St Paul's on 21 June 1675:

> a workman was sent to bring him a flat stone from a nearby heap of rubble. Wren turned it over in his hands and saw that it was a fragment of a gravestone from the old Cathedral, carved on it, in large capitals, was the single word, RESURGAM.[108]

The broken tombstone with *Resurgam* upon it can only have come from the monument to Bishop King.[109] Not only do we have Dugdale's painstaking list of all the memorials in the Cathedral, but we have its source and predecessor, Henry Holland's *Monumenta Sepulchraria Sancti Pauli*, first published in 1614, and brought up to date in 1633. Scrupulous examination of these sources proves that only one tomb in old St Paul's had the word *Resurgam* upon it, and it had nothing more. A further inscription was attached to the wall beside it, but the actual slab was otherwise plain. We know from Dugdale that this was done at Bishop King's behest, and surely, common though the use of *Resurgam* in funereal epitaphs has since become, this must have been its first appearance. Furthermore, we know how a tomb slab of 1621 might have been found broken in a pile of rubble in 1675. Dugdale tells us that the Cromwellians rifled all the tombs in the Cathedral in search of gold.

And so Bishop King's particular study and ardent faith in the Resurrection has become though the succeeding centuries the word of St Paul's:

RESURGAM

***

ACKNOWLEDGEMENTS

To the many people who have given a helping hand, in churches — Lambourne, Chiswick — in libraries, the Guildhall, Chichester Record Office, at the Fishmongers' Company and the Ironmongers' Company, I am extremely grateful. It is this free-masonry of research that makes work so enjoyable. To those who have been interested and encouraging, the Rt Revd Richard Chartres, Dame Gillian Wagner, Martin Stancliffe, John Schofield, Stephen Freeth, Penelope Hunting, Lesley Boatwright and Virginia Renner, I am deeply grateful, and thank two generations of the Antiquaries' Librarians — John Hopkins, with whom I shared the first excitement of reconnecting the picture and the pamphlets — and Bernard Nurse, for unwavering help and support. Graham Maney of Outset Services has given his best efforts to produce this work. Geremy Butler photographed the St Paul's diptych, an elusive subject. Adrian James and Kate Owen gave support from the Society of Antiquaries of London.

However, on this particular occasion my most sincere thanks must go to Christopher Whittick of the East Sussex Record Office, who has rediscovered Henry Farley's antecedents and written the biographical account of him in this book, in which he has collaborated with me throughout.

Beyond them all I must acknowledge that without the enthusiasm, the determination and guidance of Ann Saunders, this work would not have seen the light of day.

NOTES

[1] The 2001 Report by Simon Gillespie Studio for the Society of Antiquaries gives the metric measurements, 114 by 88 cm. For the first record of the picture as a possession of the Society, see Society of Antiquaries Library (hereafter SA), Minute Book **18**, 1781-2, especially 2 May 1782, pp. 152-3.

[2] The chequered history of the Society's move to Somerset House is charted by Joan Evans, *A History of the Society of Antiquaries* (Oxford, 1956), pp. 170-7.

[3] *Gentleman's Magazine* (April 1780), **50**, pp. 178-81, carries a detailed and almost entirely accurate account of this painting, to which we are indebted not only for information about the picture's provenance, but also for the suggestion (for the origin of which see below) that Farley went to Ludgate Gaol. Fragments of labels on the unpainted back of the second panel must refer to this sale in 1776.

[4] SA, Minute Book **18**, 1781-2, entry for 2 May 1782, pp. 152-3.

[5] SA, Council Minutes, 19 March 1790.

[6] T. F. Dibdin, *Aedes Althorpianae* (1822), **1**, p. 200; *Richard III*, Act 3, scene 5, line 102.

[7] J. Nichols, *The Progresses of King James the First, his Royal Consort, Family and Court* (London, 1828), IV, ii, pp. 593-6. Nichols had published an engraving of part of the procession panel as the frontispiece to this volume. His fears that the churlish treatment of the diptych would discourage other donors were unfounded. In that same year, 1828, the Society received its most important single bequest, from the Revd Thomas Kerrich.

[8] Albert Way, *Catalogue of Miscellaneous Collections in the Possession of the Society of Antiquaries of London* (1847), p. 48, no. 308. Way relied heavily on the *Gentleman's Magazine* (note 3).

[9] *A Catalogue of the Pictures belonging to the Society of Antiquaries of London*, reprinted from *The Fine Arts Quarterly Review* (1865), XLIII, pp. 32-8.

[10] *Gentleman's Magazine* (April 1780), **50**, pp. 178-81.

[11] John Donne's will, proved 5 April 1631: the National Archives, formerly Public Record Office (hereafter PRO), PROB 11/159, quire 46.

[12] Dugdale records that the stones, supplied for the repair of St Paul's as part of King James' initiative, languished in the churchyard and some of them were 'borrowed' by the Duke of Buckingham for the building of the York House watergate; Sir William Dugdale, *The History of St Paul's Cathedral*, ed. Henry Ellis (London, 1658, edition used here 1818), p. 103.

[13] The texts quoted are from J. Hayward (ed.), *John Donne: Complete Poetry and Selected Prose* (London, 1972), sermon xxx, p. 699.

[14] Ibid., pp. 738-60.

[15] St Mary Overie became Southwark Cathedral in 1905.

[16] Sir Robert Somerville, 'St Paul's Cathedral Repairs: the Propaganda of Henry Farley', in *London Topographical Record* (1985), **25**, pp. 163-75, assumed that the figures of Queen Anne and the Prince of Wales must be children since they are rendered on a smaller scale than the King. The appearance of the Queen and the Prince, however, is unmistakable. There is a profile miniature of Anne of about 1610 in the Royal Collection, illustrated by Karen Hearn (ed.), in *Dynasties: Painting in Tudor and Jacobean England 1530-1630* (Tate Gallery, 1995), p. 192 and fig. 53. The appearance of the Prince appears to have been set by an unfinished miniature by Isaac Oliver of 1615-16 (see Hearn, p. 138, no. 85). The disparity of scale between the King and his family is probably accounted for by the tradition whereby the most important persons are depicted on a larger scale than their subordinates.

[17] A preaching cross was first erected in 1241 in the area then used for the folkmoot. Thomas Kempe, Bishop of London 1448-89, rebuilt and roofed it as an outdoor pulpit. By 1483 a permanent covered gallery had been built along the north side of the choir wall to house the listeners previously sheltered by an awning. The best visual record of the pulpit and gallery is this picture. For the latest account of the pulpit and gallery, see Caroline Barron, 'London and St Paul's Cathedral in the later Middle Ages', in *Harlaxton Medieval Studies* (Donington, 2003), **10**, pp. 126-49, esp. pp. 140, 146.

[18] These quotations, with others like them, were printed in the preamble, 'Nosegay of all flowers', to Henry Farley's second pamphlet, *St Paules-Church her bill for the Parliament. As it was presented to the King's Ma[jes]tie on Midlent-Sunday last* (1621), hereafter Farley, *Bill*, unpaginated (but see note 46). Comparison with the texts of the Coverdale (1535), the Geneva (1560 and 1599 editions), the Baskett Bible and the Authorized Bible of 1611 finds the closest match in the latter, though none is exact.

[19] For the significance of 'seilled houses' at this date, see Thomas Middleton, *A Trick to Catch the Old-One* (published 1608), Act 2, scene 1, lines 291-4. In the Jacobean period 'seeling' denoted both the plastering of ceilings (then the height of fashion) and the panelling of walls or the insides of boats, see John Summerson, 'Architecture in Britain 1530-1830', in N. Pevsner (ed.), *Pelican History of Art* (Harmondsworth, 1953), p. 54.

[20] In Coverdale's version of the Bible and the Baskett Bible the word is 'beautify', as here and in the Authorized Version; in the Bishops' Bible it is 'garnish'.

[21] R. P. Crawfurd (ed.), 'The Parish Register of East Grinstead', in *Sussex Record Society* (hereafter *SRS*) (1917), **24**, pp. 29-40. The burial entries begin only in 1575 and it is possible that not all these children survived.

[22] Guildhall Library (hereafter GL), MS 5370, p. 173 or f. 60r, and F. W. Steer (ed.), 'The Scriveners' Company Common Paper, 1357-1628, with a continuation to 1678', in *London Record Society* (1968), **4**, p. 45; *Sussex Archaeological Collections* (hereafter *SAC*) (1968), **106**, pp. 51-2.

[23] His orders were noted during a visitation in 1586: West Sussex Record Office (hereafter WSRO), Ep II/11/1, f. 2v; GL, MS 9535/1, the London ordination register, confirms that ordinations took place that day but John Farley's name is not included (I am grateful to Stephen Freeth for this information); John Farley witnessed wills of parishioners in December 1572, East Sussex Record Office (hereafter ESRO), W/A 6 39, and January 1573, W/A 6 62, which he might however have undertaken merely as a neighbour. For Grindal's readiness, as Bishop of London, to ordain non-graduates, see Patrick Collinson, *Archbishop Grindal* (London, 1979), pp. 111-15; for links between Grindal and Curteys, a frequent preacher at Paul's Cross, see R. B. Manning, *Religion and Society in Elizabethan Sussex* (Leicester, 1969), pp. 70-1.

[24] The first parish register, which Farley would have been responsible for creating in 1598, has not survived; the three additional children can be identified from Clemence Farley's will, ESRO, W/A11.213.

[25] Fortune Farley (born 1563) married William Keale, tailor, son of John Keale, vicar of Kingston near Lewes, in 1584 (ESRO, PAR 408/1/1/1); Katherine Farley (born 1567) married Richard Wilson, tailor, whose will was proved in 1612 (ESRO, W/A14.8); Joan Farley (born 1570), married Richard Fitchett, probably of a tailoring family — see *SRS* (1901), **1**, p. 275.

[26] ESRO, W/A11.79.

[27] ESRO, W/A11.213, W/B3.23; ACC 2953/1, f. 77v.

[28] WSRO, Par 407/1/1/1; ESRO, OW/1603.46.

[29] ESRO, ACC 2953/1, f. 98v.

[30] Corporation of London Records Office, Archives of the City Freedom, 9 October 1605; GL, MS 5370, p. 173 or f. 60r; Steer, op. cit., p. 45; GL, MS 8721: Farley was the only scrivener among the

sixteen entered that year who had not already served an apprenticeship and been introduced by his master. No master is mentioned in Farley's case. The first scriveners to have sponsors entered in 1425. The practice became steadily more common, and after 1566 it was the general rule.

[31] Steer, op. cit., p. 59. The full membership of Godfrey Austinson, apprentice of Henry Farley, is recorded on f. 29 of Bodl. Rawl. D51, f. 29; again we are grateful to Stephen Freeth for help with this reference.

[32] Steer, op. cit., pp. 55-7, John Milton the elder, the apprentice of James Celebron, had been admitted in 1599 (Rawl. D. 51 f. 27v); in his turn he released two apprentices, William Bower and Richard Milton, in 1621 (ibid., f. 29).

[33] British Library, MS Sloane 334, ff. 4 (*Thys ys Thomas Duffyldes boke*), 301v and 302v; ESRO, W/A 7.128, W/A 9.403, DAN 1230-1236.

[34] Huntington Library, San Marino, California, MS HM 182. The capital *H*s in italics closely resemble that in Farley's signature of 1605. I am grateful to Dr Mary Robertson for assistance with this manuscript.

[35] *Gentleman's Magazine* (April 1780), **50**, pp. 178-81: 'The Deviser of this painting was one Henry Farley, who for eight years solicited and importuned the King and people with his schemes and applications for the repair of St Paul's ... This display of Master Gipkyn's art must be considered as one of the many efforts of Farley's zeal and invention to prompt his sovereign to this good and necessary work which at last brought him to Ludgate prison ...'.

[36] A statue of King Lud, the legendary founder of London, adorned the west gate of the City. Nearby lay Ludgate Prison, known in 1659 as 'King Lud's House' (Marmaduke Johnson in John Strype's edition of John Stow, *Survey of London and Westminster* (1720), Appendix 1, pp. 26-8, and by 1699 as 'Lud's Bulwark' ('B E', *Dictionary of the Canting Crew*, 1699).

[37] Probate acts granted by the Consistory Court of Chichester, the Archdeaconry of Lewes, Prerogative Court of Canterbury, the Consistory, Commissary and Archdeaconry Courts of London, the Court of Hustings, the peculiar of the Dean and Chapter of St Paul's and the Archdeaconry of Middlesex have been checked for the period between 1622, when Farley last published, and the suspension of the ecclesiastical courts in 1649, and those of the Commonwealth Court for Probate to 1660.

[38] WSRO, Par 407/1/1/1.

[39] Early in 1620 Farley applied to the secretary of the Virginia Company, 'with resolution to depart the land with speed', 'To see what savages will doe / When Christians are so hard to wooe'; it was only on the news, carried 'by a sweet Western gale of winde', of the King's imminent visit, that Farley 'forgot Virginia againe': Farley, *Bill* (1621), p. 38. The Company had sealed a new constitution for the colony on 24 July 1621: William Stithe, *History of the First Discovery and Settlement of Virginia* (New York, 1865), Appendix 4.

[40] 'A copyhold of the Bishop of Chichester's manor of Streatham', in *SAC* (1921), **62**, p. 191; P. S. Godman (ed.), 'The parish registers of Cowfold', in *SRS* (1916), p. 22.

[41] A. W. Pollard and G. R. Redgrave, *A Short Title Catalogue of Books Printed in England, Scotland and Ireland 1475-1640*, 2nd edn (London, 1986), 10688 lists copies in the British Library, Lincoln College Oxford, Lambeth Palace Library, University Library Cambridge, Trinity College Cambridge and the University of Austin, Texas.

[42] Pollard and Redgrave 13581.

[43] Ibid., 10690; copies in the British Library, Society of Antiquaries, St Paul's Cathedral Library, Bodleian, Trinity College Cambridge, Harvard Library and the Folger Shakespeare Library (imperfect). Farley makes it clear that his petition had been presented to the King on the previous Friday; whether he made a second attempt in the course of the progress is unclear. A contemporary order of the procession from the College of Arms (MS W.Y.) was printed by Dugdale, and appears again in J. Nichols, *The Progresses of King James the First, his Royal Consort, Family and Court* (London, 1828), **1**, p. 325. According to Camden, Nichols says, the procession actually went from Westminster via Temple Bar to St Paul's. The Society of Antiquaries has a contemporary manuscript with a list of participants which does not tally exactly with the one given by Nichols. It is probable these lists were drawn up in advance and not adhered to in the event. In a letter to Lord Zouch of 27 March 1620 (the following day), Sir Richard Younge wrote: 'The Prince rode bare-headed before the King, but many of the train stayed behind on disputes for presidency. The King's Councillors being unwilling to follow Earl's sons as decided by the Earl Marshall's commissioners', *Calendar of State Papers Domestic ... 1619-1623* (London, 1858), pp. 133-4.

[44] Pollard and Redgrave 10689 lists only the one copy in the British Library.

[45] These verses, and all other inscriptions on the panels, were transcribed in the *Gentleman's Magazine* (April 1780), **50**, pp. 178-81.

[46] Page 17 of the copy in the collection of the Society of Antiquaries, which I have paginated in order to facilitate reference.

[47] Farley, *Bill*, pp. 21-8.

[48] Nichols, *The Progresses of King James the First etc*, Appendix, p. 1099 prints a series of these poems, one of them in Latin and English. One of them was published by John Ashmore in *Certain Selected Odes of Horace Englished* (London, 1621), in other words in Farley's lifetime, and not at his expense.

[49] Nichols, op. cit., IV, ii, p. 593 says that Camden gave the route in 1620 from Westminster via Temple Bar.

[50] For the Union Jack on the Mary Rose, see the Anthony Roll in watercolour on vellum, completed 1546, in the Pepys Library, Magdalene College, Cambridge.

[51] J. Summerson, *Architecture in Britain 1530-1830* (Harmondsworth, 1953), p. 76, and J. Harris and G. Higgott, *Inigo Jones: Complete Architectural Drawings* (London, New York, 1989), p. 238.

[52] Farley, *Bill*, p. 27.

[53] Ibid., pp. 16-17.

[54] Somerville, op. cit. His opinion was followed in the catalogue of the exhibition, K. Wedd (ed.), *Creative Quarters: the Art World in London from 1700-2000* (Museum of London, 2001). The diptych formed the prelude to this exhibition. It was cleaned and the technique analysed by Simon Gillespie for the occasion.

[55] The project was serious. On 24 July 1604 Sir Thomas Lake, Clerk of the Signet and Latin secretary to James I, wrote to Lord Salisbury concerning the building of a new steeple, in which the King, the Lord Mayor and the Bishop were involved. On 24 October an estimate of expenses contingent thereon was £22,537 2d. For Jones' drawing, at Worcester College, Oxford, see Harris and Higgott, op. cit., pp. 38, 39 and 147 (plate).

[56] Farley, *Bill*, pp. 37-8.

[57] The pressure of a growing population can be charted in the proclamations issued by Queen Elizabeth in 1580 and 1602, and by James I between 1603 and 1625 against building new houses, or subdividing old ones, within three miles of the City gates. See Stephen Inwood, *A History of London* (London, 1998), p. 192.

[58] Caroline Barron, op. cit., note 17.

[59] Exceptions were Sir Nicholas Bacon, Lord Keeper, died 1579, who left an extremely expensive tomb, Sir William Cockain, died 1626, in whose mayoralty James I made his progress to the Cathedral, Sir Christopher Hatton, Lord Chancellor, died 1591, and the elder Sir Thomas Chaloner, died 1565. He had a house in Clerkenwell. The significant difference is that Tudor and Stuart burials entailed no provision for continued memorials.

[60] Sir William Dugdale, *The History of St Paul's Cathedral*, ed. Henry Ellis (London, 1658, edition used here 1818), p. 103.

[61] Caroline Barron, op. cit., pp. 147-8.

[62] Dugdale, op cit., p. 101.

[63] For the various ways in which this event smote the consciences of Catholics and Protestants, see Eamon Duffy, 'Bare Ruined Choirs: Remembering Catholicism in Shakespeare's England', in R. Dutton, A. Findlay and R. Wilson (eds), *Theatre and Religion* (Manchester, 2004), pp. 40-57.

[64] For Grindal as the restorer of St Paul's, see Collinson, op. cit., pp. 153-61.

[65] *SRS* (1917), **24**, pp. 35-40.

[66] Collinson, op. cit., p. 30.

[67] H. Peacham, *The Compleat Gentleman* (1622). Chaloner played an active part in negotiations between Robert Cecil and the future James I. From 1603 he was governor of Prince Henry's household. There are numerous references to him in this role in the *Calendar of State Papers Domestic* (6 August 1603, 21 December 1604, 11 December 1609). For his appointment to repair Kenilworth Castle, see under January 1606. Grants to him of land and manors appear in 1604 and of land in America in 1613. Most significantly on 9 August 1603 and 22 April and 30 June 1604 he was instrumental in identifying the Gunpowder Plot conspirators.

[68] Thomas Chaloner, *De templi divi pauli totius Angliae celeberrimi incendio*, 1561 (Pollard and Redgrave 4938.5), reprinted in *De rep[ublica] Anglorum instauranda* (London, 1579), pp. 344-5, and republished, with a translation by his friend 'LM', in John Strype (ed.), *The Survey of London* (1720), Book III, p. 149.

[69] E. Arbor, *A Transcript of the Registers of the Company of Stationers 1540-1640* (Birmingham, 1894), quoting City of London Repertory 12 (2), f. 296b or 305.

[70] C. Blair, 'Refugee Printers and Publishers in Britain during the Tudor Period', in *Proceedings of the Huguenot Society* (1970-6), **22**, pp. 115-26, esp. p. 124.

[71] Arbor, *Registers*, op. cit., **2**, p. 696.

[72] Ibid., p. 197.

[73] *Walpole Society* (1936), **24**, (*Vertue Notebooks* 4), pp. 90-1. Gipkyn's self-portrait has not been located.

[74] 'Selections from the Household Books of Lord William Howard of Naworth Castle' were published by *The Surtees Society* (1877), **68**, with an introduction by George Ormesby. References to 'Gipkyn' or 'Grinton' are recorded on pp. 73, 104, 144, 146, 148, 184, 185. E. Croft-Murray, *Decorative Painting in England 1530-1837* (London, 1962), **1**, p. 214 discusses Gipkyn's work for Naworth.

[75] Fully published by D. J. Gordon and R. Robertson, *A Calendar of Dramatic Records in the Books of the Livery Companies of London, 1485-1640 (*Malone Society Collections, 1954), **3**. Croft-Murray, op. cit., **1**, p. 214, lists the accounts from the Haberdashers' pageant, 1604, the Ironmongers' and the Grocers', all from their own records. It is in Gordon and Robertson, however, that we find all the variants on Gipkyn's name, from 'Grinton' to 'Gipking', which have prevented scholars from realizing they are all attempts to get round a foreign name and all refer to the same man.

[76] G. Wickham, *Early English Stages 1300-1660* (London, 1963), **2**, p. 337, and R. T. D. Sayle, *Lord Mayor's Pageants of the Merchant Taylors' Company in the 15th, 16th and 17th centuries* (London, 1931), pp. 87, 89, 91, 93.

[77] Wickham, op. cit., Appendix, p. 337.

[78] Gordon and Robertson, op. cit., and Sayle, op. cit., p. 87.

[79] GL, MS 5667/1, pp. 44, 46.

[80] For Edward Alleyn (1566-1626), see A. A. Reid and R. Manuira, *Edward Alleyn, Elizabethan Actor, Jacobean Gentleman* (Dulwich, 1994). This book was published to accompany an exhibition held at the Dulwich Art Gallery in the same year. I am grateful to the staff of the Dulwich Gallery and to Jan Piggott, Fellow and Archivist to the College, for help in this enquiry.

[81] These pictures are at present on loan to Tredegar House. Their documentation is set out and a selection of them illustrated in Reid and Manuira, op. cit., pp. 39-57. The sources of these extended sets of English regal portraits are elucidated by Roy Strong, *The English Icon* (Mellon, London and New York, 1969), pp. 47-8.

[82] They included, of course, Richard III. In the catalogue of *The Richard III Exhibition* at the National Portrait Gallery, 1973, portrait 24, p. 88, I discussed the classification of replicas.

[83] Reid and Manuira, op. cit., p. 54.

[84] Ibid., pp. 54-7.

[85] Reid and Manuira, op. cit., pp. 36-7; for Buckett (active 1599-1639), see also Karen Hearn (ed.), *Dynasties: Painting in Tudor and Jacobean England 1530-1630* (Tate Gallery, 1995), p. 171.

[86] Ibid., and catalogue of Alleyn's Library, p. 6, Dulwich MS V, f. 45v.

[87] *The Arches of Triumph created in honour of the high and mighty Prince James the first, King of England at His Majesty's entrance through London upon the fifteenth day of March 1603 invented and published by me, Stephen Harrison and graven by William Kip, 1604.* A copy of this sumptuous publication is in the Society of Antiquaries' Library.

[88] Karen Hearn, op. cit., p. 229 reaffirms the essential role of Norden's 1600 view as the basis of all immediately subsequent panoramas in any medium. In this she has followed Irene Scouloudi's *Panoramic Views of London 1600-1666* (London, 1953). The next view to depend upon direct observation was Wenceslaus Hollar's (1647).

[89] K. Wedd (ed), *Creative Quarters* (London, 2001), no. 1. See also Hearn, op. cit., no. 153, pp. 229-30, by far the most lucid diagnosis of this important painting and its relationship with engraved images. Hearn is right to claim the Museum of London's *London from Southwark* of *c.* 1630 as the 'earliest surviving oil painting with London as its sole subject'. However Gipkyn's first panel does attempt, if much less accurately, a section of London, and is about fifteen years earlier.

[90] Maurice Howard, 'Classicism and Civic Architecture in Renaissance England', in L. Gent (ed), *Albion's Classicism: the Visual Arts in Britain* (Yale, 1995), pp. 29-49, esp. p. 35.

[91] The text is published in Nichols' *Progresses*, op. cit., **II**, pp. 679-97.

[92] I have published the evidence in the thirteenth-century Wells Cathedral and fourteenth-century Exeter Cathedral. For Wells and Salisbury, see L. Colchester (ed.), *Wells Cathedral, a History* (Shepton Mallet, 1982), pp. 116-20. For Exeter, see M. Swanton (ed.), *Exeter Cathedral — a Celebration* (Exeter, 1991), pp. 137-43.

[93] L. Grenade, *Les Singularitéz de Londres, 1576*, see Ann Saunders (ed.), *The Royal Exchange* (London Topographical Society, 1997), pp. 48-9.

[94] The Cheapside in which this comedy and through which Gipkyn's procession moves is vividly evoked in John Schofield, *Medieval London Houses* (New Haven and London, 1994). On p. 73 he describes a survey of 1617 of a property in Cheapside rebuilt in 1595.

[95] Thomas Middleton, *A Chaste Mayd in Cheap-side* (first performed at the Swan, probably in 1613, and published 1630), Act 5, scene 1, lines 165-74. From Brian Loughrey and Neil Taylor (eds), *Five Plays: Thomas Middleton* (Harmondsworth, 1988). Cf. also Richard Dutton (ed.), *Thomas Middleton: Women Beware Women and other plays* (Oxford, 1999), p. xxi of introduction.

[96] In Irish bardic tradition a vision is called an 'aisling'. Striking contemporary use of the form is made by Brian O'Doherty in *The Deposition of Father McGreevy* (London, 1999), p. 307: 'I had fallen asleep in my room and had a dream in which I found myself on a grassy bank by a river under a flowering tree and fell asleep again. In this second sleep I was visited by a vision ...'. Normally the vision would be of a female personification of Ireland. Could the 'ferly' in *Piers Plowman* be the English equivalent of an 'aisling'? Is the idea of a vision within a dream the key to Farley's contradictions?

[97] This quotation is from J. B. Trapp, 'Medieval English Literature', in F. Kermode and J. Hollander (eds), *The Oxford Anthology of English Literature* (Oxford, 1973), p. 352.

[98] During the recent conservation a pricked outline was observed round one of the flying angels in the third panel. It is possible Gipkyn traced his first angel, and then pricked out the rest from it, reversing the paper for the angels on the other side of the spire. Alternatively he may have used an engraving for all the angels. The source is not known.

[99] F. C. Penrose, 'Recent Discoveries of Portions of Old St Paul's', in *Archaeologia* (1883), **47**, esp. plate xiii and pp. 381-90. Even in its present disposition the north-eastern angle of St Paul's acts as a natural sounding board for a speaker on the site of Paul's Cross.

[100] For the history of Paul's Cross, rebuilt by Thomas Kempe, Bishop of London (1448-89), and the covered gallery, see Caroline Barron, op. cit., pp. 140-1.

[101] In the painting he has used the royal box as a vehicle for further inscriptions. Beneath the seated figures there are inscribed 'Vive le Roi', 'Vive la Reine' and 'Vive le Prince'. Under the seats for lords, ladies and Bishops is written 'Mr. William Parker, Citizen and Merchant Taylor, gave 400 pounds towards repairs of my windows': Farley, *Bill*, p. 18.

[102] Dugdale, op. cit.

[103] *Calendar of State Papers Domestic, James I, 1619-23* (London, 1858), p. 132, 21 March 1620.

[104] J. Earle, *Micro-Cosmographie, or a Poem of the World discovered in Essays and Characters* (William Stansby for Edward Blount, 1628), see *English Reprints* (London, 1869), p. 73.

[105] Dugdale, op. cit., p. 106 note.

[106] See Francis Blomfield's *Norfolk* (1805-10), **8**, pp. 423-4, and Francis Steer in *The Essex Review* (January 1944), **53**, no. 209, p. 2; I am grateful to Canon Paul Allton of Gaywood and his photographer for information and photographs. The picture was borrowed for the Armada Exhibition, Greenwich (1988), catalogue by David Cordingley.

[107] Pollard and Redgrave 14976.

[108] This tale is told whenever the rebuilding of St Paul's is recounted. It appears, for example, in P. Burman, *St Paul's Cathedral* (New Bell's Cathedral Guides, London, 1987), pp. 42-3.

[109] The association of *Resurgam* with Bishop King's tomb was suggested by Sister Hilary in her lecture on John Donne given as a Lent lecture on seventeenth-century spirituality at Sion College, 28 March 1988, and reference was made to it in the Very Revd Alan Webster's Easter sermon in St Paul's the same year. I am grateful to Sister Hilary for letting me see the text of her lecture, and to Alan Webster for discussing it with me. I thank also Rosemary Cockayne for drawing my attention to this previous airing of the source of *Resurgam*. *Resurgam* became a very popular word on tomb stones. By the nineteenth century it was so familiar as to be the basis of an anecdote by Anthony Trollope in his novel *Doctor Thorne* (1858), chapter iv.

TOPOGRAPHICAL AND HISTORICAL NOTES

By ANN SAUNDERS

Henry Farley's objective was the restoration of St Paul's Cathedral and the replacement of its spire. We may assume that to this good purpose he financed the painting of the diptych and the printing of his three appeals, *The Complaint of Paules*, 1616, *St Paules-Church her bill for the Parliament*, 1621, and *Portland-Stone in Paules-Church-yard*, 1622, the first and third of which we republish here.

In these poems, he provides us with an extraordinary, unexploited and truly personal source of information about the streets, sights and politics of early seventeenth-century London.

We may examine them first for a contemporary description of the lamentable condition of the Cathedral. The venerable building is made to tell of its misfortune.

> To loose my toppe, a stately, *princely spire*,
> By lightening, which set the same on fire,
> And burnt it downe, (a wonderfull mishap)
> Leaving me bare and bald without a cappe,
> Like an old shippe without her masts and sayles,
> Having no *Beautie*, but poore rotten rayles.

In *Portland-Stone* (pp. 25–7), Farley cries out against the misuse of the sacred building:

> Was it not example scurrilous and rude,
> At first to grant that trades should there intrude;
> Nay are they not accursed, that did yeeld
> To make Gods Courts a merchandizing field?
> May we not call them beasts, even to their faces,
> That like bruit beasts defile such sacred places?
>
> Shold *Christians bones* be dig'd out of their graves
> And laid with dogs bones in the fields by knaves
> That so more roome under the Church foundation
> May be for *A-iaxe* in a beastly fashion?
> No easment but again the Temple wals [*sic*]?
> No other place to pisse, or make Laystals?
> No waye to passe with burthens, but throgh *Pauls*
> wher burthend consciences shold ease their soules?

Having made clear the Cathedral's parlous condition, Farley's *Complaint* contrasts it with the handsome, modern estate of the rest of London. Twice (pp. 9 and 35) he refers to the new steeple of St Mary-le-Bow in Cheapside, 'verie well beautified at the cost of one Parish', and speaks of

> ...the shaft or spire that should bee best,
> But that's upon *S. Dunstanes* in the *East*
> (*Complaint*, p. 35)

London, the 'fairest Citie in this land', glows in his pages; his report is up to the minute, for he speaks with approval of 'the garden call'd Th'artilarie', where the members of what is today the Honourable Artillery Company practise their arms and drill in Spitalfields. You can see the scene clearly on *The A to Z of Elizabethan*

London (1979, LTS Publication No. 122, p. 11); the Company did not acquire its present headquarters and ground in Finsbury until 1641.

He also comments approvingly on London's water supply – 'The River which was cut the other day' – for the New River, engineered by Sir Hugh Myddelton to bring fresh water from Amwell in Hertfordshire to Clerkenwell, had been declared open as recently as September 1613 by the Lord Mayor, brother to the entrepreneur.

Farley's reporting is up to the minute. The poem was written within a year of the paving and chaining of Smithfield Market:

> From thence to *Smithfield* if thou chance to hit,
> Tell me what costs they have bestow'd on it,
> It was before a filthy noisome place,
> And to the *Citie* verie much disgrace,
> Yet now some say it may with best compare,
> Of market places that in England are.
>
> (*Complaint*, p. 9)

His remark about the Globe Theatre on the opening page of his book demonstrates his topicality:

> For I have seene the Globe burnt,
> and quickly made a Phoenix.

The theatre of Burbage and Shakespeare had been accidentally destroyed by fire on 29 June, 1613; the mortar can scarcely have been dry on the new building before Farley slips in his comment. He boasts of London's charitable support of those in need:

> Also for *Charitie* and good *Almes-deedes*,
> What *Citie* under *heaven* more poore feeds?
> Or who more bountifull to *Preachers* be,
> Then [sic] Londiners to their abilitie?
>
> (*Complaint*, p. 10)

He praises Sir Thomas Sutton for his generosity:

> One such a *Sutton* as of late did die,
> That turned *Charter-house* to *charitie*.
> . . .
> But such a worthy *Phoenix* is so rare,
> That hardly any will with him compare.
>
> (*Complaint*, p. 36)

Farley has a shrewd eye for misbehaviour. He is particularly critical of those who cheat and waste time in building work:

> Some men there are will maintain to ones face,
> (But such we hold both lewd and very base)
> That in a worke for King or Church they may
> Trifle the time by loytring and delay...
>
> Some with their Rules do sidle up and downe,
> As if they did more worke then all the towne:
> But mark them wel & give them their due check
> For one weeks work, almost three daies they lack.
>
> (*Portland-Stone*, pp. 33–4)

Farley's attitude to the royal family is as interesting as his comments on the capital; they have an air as gushing and as fulsome as some twenty-first century weekly magazine. James is always 'England's Salomon', his consort Anne of Denmark is

> Best *Queene of Women* for Best King of Man.
>
> (*Complaint*, p. 3)

He remembers the recently deceased Prince Henry, while Charles, now heir to the throne, is

> …our joy and treasure
> Whom all true subjects love in boundlesse measure
>
> (*Complaint*, p. 4)

He becomes lyrical when he writes of Princess Elizabeth, married three years before to Frederick, Elector Palatine, whom we know as the Winter Queen, in remembrance of her few months' sovereignty over Bohemia.

> *Rhynes* sweete *Princesse, Brittaines joy,*
> *Holding in her armes a Boy,*
> Whom (if Art doe not dissemble)
> *Her first borne He did resemble*
>
> (*Complaint*, p. 62)

The baby is Prince Maurice, whose younger brother will be Rupert of the Rhine, Charles I's general during the Civil War. Farley includes the Queen's brother, Christian IV of Denmark, and does not forget James' and Anne's two dead infants, Mary and Sophia, who lie in Innocents' Corner in Westminster Abbey. Such affection and admiration for the monarch and his family make Farley's somewhat clumsy lines poignant when we know that the Civil War is only a quarter of a century away.

One other contemporary reference is worth noticing. Three times does Farley mention Virginia in his *Complaint*, on pages 29, 30, and 33. There had been two unsuccessful attempts, in 1585 and 1587, during Elizabeth's reign, to colonize the New World; new companies were incorporated in 1606 and fresh attempts fared better. His name, so far, remains untraced, but we may wonder whether Farley did not make the voyage across the Atlantic. His chief memorial remains his crusade to restore St Paul's, through both his writings and the diptych.

APPENDIX 1

In Appendices 1 and 2 we have tried to reproduce the text of Farley's poems as accurately as possible without attempting a facsimile. To facilitate the finding of references, numerical sequence of pages is given in square brackets. In Appendix I from p.60 [p.64] onwards, Farley's typesetter is unreliable in his enumeration.

[p.1]

THE
COMPLAINT
OF PAULES,
TO
ALL CHRISTIAN
SOULES:

OR an humble Supplication,
To our good King and Nation,
For Her newe Reparation.

Written by HENRIE FARLEY.

Amore, Veritate, & Reverentia.

Printed by CANTRELL LEGGE.
1 6 1 6.

[p.2]

The Booke to the
Reader.

If you will judge me, (my good friend)
First reade me thorough to the ende,
If all be well, you may commend me,
If ought amisse, I pray amend me.

For every one should gladly doe,
The same he would be done unto.

[p.3]

I Poore *Paules* dejected and distressed, yet beeing in the best prospect, and taller then all my fellowes) doe see, or at least may see, (if my windowes be eyes) many stately monuments, houses, and other things builded, and done within these fewe yeeres, some for Honour, some for profit, some for Beautie, some for pleasure, some for health and recreation, some for Royall entertainments and sports, and many for charitable uses:

And I have seene the Globe burnt, and quickly
made a Phœnix.

Q. But who sees me?   A. Who sees thee not?

Tunc etiam spero,

And hope will still, though still I have the worst ;
For wer't not for some hope, my Heart would burst.

[p.4]

Before the Complaint *is added*

a Prologue, *and after the same an* Epilogue, *and a* Dreame.

1. T*He* Prologue, *is a charge given by the* Church *to this* Booke; *namely, that it should disperse it selse to the* Court, Clergie, Cities, *and* Countries, *to search and finde out all such as are* Royally, Graciously, Honourably, Religiously, Vertuously, Charitably, *and* Bountifully *minded towards the repaire thereof, To the ende* (that Their *lights shining in such a* glorious worke of Pietie) *may thereby illuminate, and inflame the hearts of all others, to be willing* Benefactors, Contributors, *and* Coadiutors *to the same.*

2. The Epilogue *discovereth a* Iew-rie *of* Knights of the Post; *that in this, and in all other* Pious Designes, *will ever sweare to the contrarie.*

3. The Dreame *is a* Vision *which the* Author *saw in his sleepe, shewing the manner and fashion, how (as he thought) the said* Church and steeple *were beautified and repaired.*

[p.5]

1

THE PROLOGUE.

And first to the Court.

F L I E little Booke, from East unto the West,
From North to South, or where thou likest best,
Search *Brittaine* out, in all *Her* better parts,
Amongst the *Noblest*, and the *Worthiest* hearts.
But first (as dutie bindeth) take thy wing,
And flie to *Faiths Defender*, J A M E S *my King;*
Beseech *His Highnesse,* (by all meanes that bee)
That (*as S. Albons*) He would pittie mee,
And so to order, by *His* Great command,
That I may be repaired out of hand;
Else I shall weare away, and cracke, and fall,
To my great sorrow, and my lovers all.
OH tell *His Majestie* in humble sort,
That thou art come unto *His Royall Court*

[p.6]

2   ***First, to the Court.***

To begge a Boon', that never beg'd before,
Which (if *Hee* graunt) thou never shalt begge more;
And be thou sure before from *Him* thou part,
Thou get Compassion from *His Kingly Heart;*
Like as the woman was to *Christ*, to be
Importunate unto his *Majestie.*
Doe not thou looke, like one, that will bee daunted,
But pray, and speake, untill my suite be graunted;
And say, Although I ragged am, and torne,
As if I were, to all the rest a scorne;
Yet *Christendome* thr'oughout can truely tell,
That I for *Name* and *Fame* doe beare the Bell;
And ner'thelesse that I am call'd poore *Paules*,
I feed (*with th' choicest delicates*) more *Soules,*
Then any Three (the greatest *Churches*) doe,
In *England*, and in all *Great Brittaine* too.
And when thou hast thus labour'd *Him* a while,
Marke, if *His Gracious Countenance* doe smile:
For if it doe, be sure *Hee* doth affect thee,
And with *His Royall favour* will protect thee;
And by *His sacred wisedome*, will devise
A speedy way for my *Re-edifice.*

[p.7]

3   ***First, to the Court***

So I shall have just cause this song to sing,
No grace in th' earth to that of God and King;
And shortly will be sung by every infant,
That good King JAMES made me againe Triumphant.

T H E N goe to *Her*, whose *Princely vertues* shine
As if *shee* were a *Goddesse* most Divine,
(I meane my *Gracious Queene* and *Lady* A N N E,
Best *Queene of Women*, for Best *King of Man*:)
Beseech that *Peereles Paragon of Time*,
That *Shee* will daigne t' accept thy honest Rime;
The rather, in respect *Her Royall Brother,*
Was the *Prime cause thereof*, not any other,
Who beeing (in the sight of many people)
With other famous *Princes* on my steeple,
My *Writer* did conceit, *His Highnesse* spake
Some charitable motion for my sake,
That it were charges well bestowed and spent,
To doe me Grace with some faire Ornament;
As with a *Crowne*, a *Spire*, or some good thing,
More fitter for to entertaine a *King.*
And 'cause *Hee* there did print *His royall foote,*

[p.8]

4   ***First, to the Court***

Poore man suppos'd *Hee* sign'd and seald unto't:
And say I what I can, yet is his Creed,
His Highnesse did deliver't as *His Deed*:
In which conceit (though oftentimes restrain'd)
Hee could not rest, till thus I had complain'd.
   OH tell *Her Highnesse* that *Her Ladyes faire,*
Would give good gifts to see my newe repaire,
And that, if first *Her Majestie* beginne,
All *Worthies* of *her sexe* will then come in,
And bring *their Angels, Nobles, and their Crownes,*
From *Cities, Countries, Villages,* and *Townes;*
For Women never were of better spirits,
To doe the workes that *Fame* and *honour* merits,
Then now they are, God graunt them be so still,
Patternes of good, and haters of all ill. *amen.**

A N D when thou hast appear'd to *King* and *Queene,*
Unto their *Princely Sonne* likewise be seene,
The high and mightie C H A R L E S, our joy and treasure,
Whom all true subjects love in boundlesse measure.
   Say to this *Worthy, Welbeloved Prince,*
It was my chance some fiftie five yeares since,

* ms addition

[p.9]

5 ***First, to the Court.***

To loose my toppe, a stately *princely spire*,
By lightening, which set the same on fire;
And burnt it downe, (a wonderfull mishap,)
Leaving me bare and bald without a cappe,
Like an old shippe without her masts and sayles,
Having no *Beautie*, but poore rotten rayles.
　　Pray tell this *Prince* what *honour* it will bee
Unto *His Highnesse* if *Hee* speake for me ;
And what a *Glory, Name*, and *Fame*, and *praise*,
Unto *Great Brittaine* it will ever raise,
If this my humble suit be well respected,
That so with speede the worke may be effected.

So from the *Prince* (as fast as thou are able,)
Make hast to goe unto the *Counsell Table*,
Shewe wherefore thou do'st come, and make a motion,
Unto their *Honours* there for their Devotion;
That *They'le* be pleas'd to joyne with *Majestie*,
In such a worke of *Christian Pietie* ;
I knowe *Their Wisedomes* and *Their Worths* are such,
They will in this no *gift* nor *counsell* grutch.

[p.10]

6 ***First, to the Court.***

T H E N to all other *Lords* and *Ladies* bright,
And every *vertuous Gentleman and Knight*,
Doe thou appeare; and say th'art come from me,
And I doe hope thou shalt more welcome bee:
As sure as I in *famous London* stand,
I shall have gifts of every *Noble* hand.

A N D when with *Lords* and *Ladies* thou hast done,
About the *House* in every office runne,
And from the highest to the lowest Groome,
Say, thou for my repaire and helpe art come,
And I dare wager every one will say,
They'le give to me, and spare another way.

Secondly, to the Clergie.

T H U S doe thou leave the *Court*, and quickly hie
Unto the Reverend Bishops and Clergie,
And giving *Them* due *Grace and Reverence*,
Crave thou *Their Bounties* and *Benevolence*.

[p.11]

7 ***Secondly, to the Clergie.***

　　Tell *Them* I am *Their Church* of greatest note,
Although I weare a poore and ragged coate;
And stand in fairest *Citie* of this Land,
And with great state was builded to *Their* hand.
I was the onely *Mirrour*, so am still,
But then for *Beautie*, now for *looking ill*:
And *Strangers* wonder, why I am so bare,
Where such great costs on pleasures buildings are:
And where for *Vanitie*, there wants no coine,
Or any thing to make *her* brave and fine.
　　I doe assure *them* (under *their* Correction)
That I have lived long in great subjection,
And 'cause I doubt my rents and meanes are small,
That I shall not be mended till I fall,
I thinke it not amisse for *Them* and mee,
To trie what helpe from others there will bee:
So I have turn'd thee to the world therefore,
That (if I want,) *good men* may give me more:
And doubtlesse there are *Thousands* that would give,
Great and large gifts, to see me prosperous live.

[p.12]

8 ***Thirdly, to the Citie.***

N O W from the *Clergy* walke through *London-City*,
And looke them out that my poore case do pitie;
For there thou'lt finde innumerable many,
That for my good, will doe as much as any;
No place so *famous* as that *Royall Towne*,
For works of *Worth*, of *Honour*, and *Renowne*.
Be it for profit, pleasure, health, or state,
(Whatsoe're it cost,) the Citizens will ha't.
　　Marke but *Morefields*, how it's advanced hie
That did before both lowe and loathsome lie:
And going on take *Algate* in thy way,
Note well *her* building, and *her* rich aray.
Then without feare of stocks or pillorie,
Goe to the *garden* call'd *Th' artilarie*,
Passe by the *pikes* and *muskets*, and be bold,
That *honourable action* to behold:
And I am sure if backe thy newes thou bring,
Thou wilt protest it is a *worthy* thing,

[p.13]
9 ### *Thirdly, to the Citie.*

That *men of note* their time and coine should spend,
To practise *Armes,* their *Country* to defend,
And voluntarily themselves incline,
To learne the rules of *Martiall discipline.*
       I like it wondrous well, and could agree,
In every *Shire* and *Towne* the like might bee,
That if in time we come to counterbuffes,
We may have skill at *Armes* more then at cuffes,
And be prepar'd with skill and armour bright,
Against *Gods* enemies, and mine to fight.
       Nowe come to *Bowe* in *Cheape* that cost full deare,
And see how gloriously shee doth appeare.
       From thence to *Smithfield* if thou chance to hit,
Tell me what costs they have bestow'd on it ,
It was before a filthy noisome place,
And to the *Citie* verie much disgrace,
Yet now some say it may with best compare,
Of market places that in England are.
       Then unto *Amwell* see what you can say,
(The *River* which was cut the other day,)
Me thinkes it is a very famous thing,
And doth much comfort to the *Citie* bring:

[p.14]
10 ### *Thirdly, to the Citie.*

I needs must say it doth, and will avowe it,
And so I thinke all others will allow it,
And praise the *Founders* for their good intention,
And pray to blesse *them,* and their newe invention.
       So may you verie well the *Founders* praise,
Of *water-engins* made in former dayes;
For they are worthy, and their works good still,
Though *Amwell* doe the best it can or will.
       Also for *Charitie* and good *Almes-deedes,*
What *Citie* under *heaven* more poore feeds?
Or who more bountifull to *Preachers* be,
Then *Londiners* to their abilitie?
       All which I doe, and may rejoyce to see,
And hope (in time*)* they'le doe some good to mee:
And so will leave a thousand things to name,
That likewife doe deserve their lasting fame,
And those more cheifely which were done of late,
(Together with their triumphs of great state,)
Because for thee my *Booke,* and for the *Wise,*
I hope t'will be enough for to suffice.
       And therefore nowe thy dutie there is done,
See that to other Cities thou be gone;

[p.15]
11 ### *Fourthly, to the Countrie.*

Intreat *them* faire as thou go'st on thy way,
And doe not care what carping Critticks say.

Fourthly, to the Countrie.

W H E N thou hast done in *Citie* and in *Towne,*
I pray thee walke the *Countries* up and downe,
And so disperse thy selfe both farre and wide,
Till every honest Christian heart be tride:
Spare neither *sexe,* nor *age,* nor *bond,* nor *free,*
Nor any one of whatsoe're degree:
For though some places are but poore and bare,
Yet will the poorest have a mite to spare;
The Countrie welcome I doe knowe is kind,
Where meanes doth hit according to the minde.
       Therefore my loving *Booke* take heart and goe,
Thou shalt finde tenne good friends for one bad foe:
Doe not thou feare for want of *Eloquence*
Or filed tearmes, to please the outward sence;
But with a courage and a conscience free,

[p.16]
12 ### *Fourthly, to the Countrie.*

Doe what thou canst to grace and pleasure me,
And I will pray as much as in me is
To bring my Benefactors unto blisse,
Thy words are honest, and thy matter true,
Wherefore goe on I say, and so *A-Dieu.*

Thy wel-willer to the
Worlds ende,
S^t. P A U L E S Church.

[p.17]
13

The Epistle of the Author to
all Courteous and Charitable Readers.

I F you should aske me *Why* I undertooke,
Into the ruines of *Paules Church* to looke?
Or *How* I durst (like Bayard) lift my Muse,
To such a height, or such a subject chuse?
Or *Who* provok'd me on, or bid me doe it?
Or who did set their helping hands unto it?
Or *Which* way I doe thinke this Land can raise,
Inough *Benevolence* in these hard dayes?
Or *What* the ende of my intent should be?
Or *When* I thought this worthy worke to see?
To these your *Why,* your *How, Who, Which, What, When,*

I answer thus kind friends and Gentlemen:
First, for your *Why*, my reason I will tell,
It's cause I love, and still will love *Bethel*;
And *How* I durst on such a subject write?
It's cause I doe it in the Churches right;
For whom, and for my Prince and Countrie too,
I'le spend my blood, write, speake, ride, runne, or go.

[p.18]
14   ***To the Courteous Reader.***

And for your *Who* did bid me or assist me?
It was my God that hitherto hath blist me.
And for your *Which* way such great gifts will rise,
I could set presidents before your eyes
Of one or two, whose deeds so farre extend,
As would build three, and this Church well amend.
Then wonder not (I pray) which way or whence,
This Land should raise such great *Benevolence*.
And for your *What's* the ende of my intention ?
The scope of all my Booke will make you mention.
And lastly, for your *When* this worke shall bee,
Belongs unto my *Betters* not to me,
To *God* and *King*, and *Powr's superiour*,
And not to me that am inferiour.

   Wherefore (*good Readers*) take it well in worth,
The answer which to you I have set forth,
And when this *Booke* of mine abroad is sent,
(Though poore and plaine) beleeve it is well meant:
And ev'ry thing's well done that's taken so,
But otherwise the good for bad doth goe.

   I doe confesse and all the world may know-it,
I am too weake, to have the name of *Poet*,

[p.19]
15   ***To the Courteous Reader.***

Yet I protest I like so well the art,
I would a good one bee withall my heart;
But now it is too late to wish or crie
I was no *poet* borne nor one shall die.

   Since first into this business I waded,
I could not be by any friend disswaded,
Although they told me strange things of these dayes,
That might have made me doubtfull many wayes;
But beeing voide of feares, or thought of harme,
I did my selfe with Christian courage arme,
And stoutly went through thicke and thinne to shore,
Where never any waded yet before;
And now have finisht what my *soule* requir'd,
Though not so well by halfe as I desir'd;
God graunt it may such good acceptance have,
That once againe this *Bethel* may be brave.
And you deare *Friends* whose favours I obtaine,

Health to your dayes while here you doe remaine,
And after this life ever may you stand,
Most blesed *Saints* in the *Celestiall Land*.

       Yours onely in the uttermost of my
                   best endeavours and wishes,
           H E N R I E F A R L E Y.

[p.20]
16

At *Zoilus, Momus,* and their mates, This doe I fling to breake their pates.

*C*Ritticks surcease, and doe not stirre too much,
Least medling more then needs, I may you touch,
And tell you to your teeth you are no friends
To any good beginnings, or good ends.
Though plaine I am, to Prince *I am as true,*
And loyall *too, as are the proud'st of you:*
Nor have I wronged you or any other,
More then a loving child would wrong his mother:
Or written anything so voide of reason,
But that it may (to good men) come in season:
Wherefore let Justice *rule you, and be quiet,*
And seeke not 'gainst my right to make a riot:
For if you doe, I must defend my cause,
By helpe of God, or King, or Armes, or Lawes;
Yet will I yeeld my life unto my Betters,
But not to you, if I should starve in fetters.

[p.21]
17

   Perhaps I'm borne to bee a Phinees *bold,*
To begge and pray for poore, and weake and olde,
And such as are both dumbe, and deafe, and blind,
That in this flintie Age no helpe can ffind.

   What's that to you, or wherefore should you grutch,
When nine times worse, you spend ten times as much?
But that's to please your humour, that's well done,
And in that vaine your course runnes headlong on,
Untill you make your selves so poore and bare,
That twentie such have not a doite *to spare.*

   If this my suite be rightly well regarded,
I may have thanks, and love, and be rewarded:
And more then that, (if lucke do not miscarrie)
Paules friends will say, I was an honest Harry:
So gaine a vertuous Fame *when I am rotten,*
By future Ages *not to be forgotten,*
While (if you please) you may goe shooe the goose,
And (wanting garters) weare your stockings loose.

           Yours, as you plainly see,
           till you are friends with mee.
                       H. F.

[p.22]
18

___

In laudem Authoris
Carmen ɛηκωμιαϛικον

___

SEmiruta aspiciens Paulini culmina templi
Farleius, queritur tale perire decus.
Mox pia spirantem componit vota libellum,
Et quia non poterat magna, minora facit.
Qui si tam nosset templum, quam condere versum,
Efficeret propria, quod vovet, ipse manu.
Fortunet laetis deus hoc successibus ausum,
Gloria & ingenuum certa sequatur opus.*

___

The great *Kings* House, & Courts on earth decay
Let *King,* and *Court* to heaven raise up againe,
And of the *Church-men* let it ner'e be said,
That they did grudge the *Temple* to maintaine:
Let *London Londons* beauty beautifie,
And *Countrie-men* their *Countries*-dignity:
And with the Churches wished exaltation,
Mount up this Authors rightfull commendation.

I.W. T.C.

___

*Song of Praise

Seeing the ruinous vaults of Paul's church,
Farley laments that such glory is perishing.
Soon he composes a pamphlet breathing pious vows,
And unable to achieve the greater, achieves the lesser [task].
If he had known how to build a temple as well as build verses
He would have accomplished with his own hand what he vows.
May God prosper this venture with joyful successes
And may sure glory attend the noble work.

The verse is written in elegiac couplets in a reasonably elegant
style. The identity of its author must rest upon the initials at the
bottom of the page. *TC* almost certainly represents Thomas
Chaloner, who had died on 15 November 1615, the year before
publication. *IW* is harder to identify, and only further research
will determine whether it might stand for John Winniffe (died
1630), the father of the Dean of St Paul's in whose Essex
rectory the diptych came to light in the eighteenth century.

[p.23]
19

THE
COMPLAINT OF
Pː AULES,
TO ALL CHRISTIAN
SOULES.

THE great complaint that here is made good people,
Is of *Pauls Church,* and of that polled steeple,
Which stands within the famous citie London,

Cracked, defaced, rent, and almost undone:
Mourning like *Charing-crosse,* be'ing much decaid,
And of the stormes and winter blasts afraid,
Saying (alas) will no man pitie me,
But suffer still my poore adversitie?
    I'st *S. Pauls doctrine* you would faine imbrace?
Then crowne my head, do me some outward *Grace:*
Let strangers see and all that come to Towne,
That your cheife Church doth flourish, not fall downe:
And let me have some *Beautie,* forme, and fashion,

[p.24]
20   ***The Complaint of Paules,***

That yee may shewe your selves a loving *Nation,*
And so assure me you doe not reject me,
But with your wonted favours doe respect me.

    I know that for your owne delights and pleasures,
Upon your houses you bestow great treasures,
Without, within, not any costs you spare,
To make them shew most beautifull and rare,
With stately *Lanthornes, Pyramids,* and things ,
Pictures of mightie *Emperours* and *Kings,*
High *turrets, towers* and curious phanes of price,
As if it were the place of *Paradise,*
While I am bare, and like a *Chaos* stand,
That should be fairest prospect in the land.

    What is the reason I should be no higher?
Because my chance was to be burnt with fire:
Or doe you thinke the charge but cast away
That is bestowed on the Church decay?
Or is it *Merlins* sorceries and lies
Hath made you feare with his false *prophesies* ?
Or what's the reason you should thus neglect
To build me up againe with faire prospect?

[p.25]
21   ***to all Christian soules.***

    I am *Gods house,* consider then I pray,
What cause there is that I should thus decay:
Is it not pitty I should ragged bee,
While on proud flesh such golden gawdes I see?
    Alas for shame I cannot choose but blush,
To see the world so stumble at a rush,
Yet easily it skips and leaps or'e blocks,
Not sparing charge, nor fearing any knocks.
    A thousand yeeres I stood in prosperous state,
And so remained till it was of late:
My auncient *Founders* were my lovers deare,
They spar'd no cost as doth full well appeare:
But rais'd me from the ground aloft the skies,
To be a wonder for a world of eyes,
And made my watchfull cocke stretch forth his wings,

As doth the *Larke* when (mounting high) he sings
Haleluiah with his pretie voice,
And (neer'st the Heavens,) more he doth rejoyce.
   Then with the least aire that in skie did blowe,
Which way the winde did set, my cocke would showe;
Ah, then was I a *Princely Monument*,
In sight of all that unto *London* went:

[p.26]
22   *The Complaint of Paules,*

And then had I the *Commendation*,
And held in highest reputation:
But now (like one forlorne,) I stand unpitt'ed,
As if I had some monstrous fault committed.
   Sometimes a view is made upon my wants,
And then (twixt hope and feare) my heart it pants,
But all in vaine I hope, (alas my griefe,)
Surveyours gone, then this is my releife;
To undertake so high a worke to mend,
Great is the charge (saie some) and to no end,
For (but for shew) to what use will I serve,
Whereby such cost on mee, I should deserve?
Which censure makes me linger in consumption,
That to bee cured I have small presumption.
   Fie, fie, where are the minds were heretofore?
Are they growne poore, and will be rich no more?
Or are the gold and silver Ages past,
And now an iron Age, left at the last?
      Then woe is mee, my hopes, are fond and vaine,
      I never looke to be repair'd againe,
   When first I was by *Ethelbert* beganne,
No helpe was wanting could be found in man;

[p.27]
23   *to all Christian Soules.*

The Labre'r would beginne at worke to sweate,
Before he did desire to drinke or eate;
All workmen strived for to shewe their skill,
Not so much for their gaine, as in good will;
Whether by taske, or working by the day,
Not one that would a minute spend in play;
Nor would they sleight their workes as now men doe,
But wrought with Art and expedition too;
One free dayes worke in every weeke I knowe,
They would on me most willingly bestowe.
   What should I say? If I should goe about,
To reckon all particulars throughout;
(The rules observed to beginne and ende,
The gifts that many unto mee did send,
The solemne orders laying my first stone,
With hallowing the ground I stand upon:
The candles that were burned every night,
At everie time I grewe a man in height,

The noise of *Drummes* and eke of *Trumpets* sound,
When first I did appeare above the ground;
The *triumph* made at my first *Scaffolds* raise,
The *solemne songs* were sung in *Heavens* praise:

[p.28]
24   *The Complaint of Paules,*

The number set on worke by sea and land ,
As if the Christian world I might command;
   If I were best that useth swift to write,
   I could not in two yeeres the same recite.
And if so many men were in a plaine,
As for my good did labour and take paine,
A *royall armie* would appeare to be ,
Of power to fight with mightie enemie.
They wrought about me like the prettie bees,
And every night went home with wearie knees,
And every morne came fresh to worke againe,
As if the day before they felt no paine:
Their honey-drops distill'd from them apace,
(I meane the sweate of every workemans face)
Their labour was their festivall for me,
In hope my future prosperous state to see,
   A world it was to note how all were bent,
How willingly their coyne and time they spent,
Without a Lotary or forc'd collection.
For all were free in any such good action:
There was no pining at the Church expence,
But all was brought in true Benevolence:

[p.29]
25   *to all Christian soules.*

And those that died in my *diocesse*,
Would will me something, more or lesse:
At all communions, and marriage dayes,
At Christenings, and many other waies:
The very poorest, would (without excuse)
Send or give something to my proper use:
And all to make mee beautifull and faire,
That Christ his *flocke* might unto me repaire,
To teach and learne the *Heavenly* words of Grace,
And so to growe and fructifie apace,
In all good waies of Christian *Pietie*,
Best pleasing to the *Heavenly Deitie*.
Which (in good time) is long since brought to passe,
The like as ner'e in any kingdome was:
So that for preaching, I may now compare
With all the Churches under heaven are.
   Praised be *God* whose goodnesse doth excell,
Beyond what I can aske, or tongue can tell,
From age to age, hee still hath succour'd mee,
And out of thrall for ever set me free.
   My inward garments, shine so bright and pure,
As now no errour can the same obscure:

[p.30]
26   ***The complaint of Paules,***

For on the *Bread of life* in me you feede,
And doe receive all things your soules doe neede;
My *Preachers* bid you come, buy without money,
Things sweeter then the honey-combe or honey;
They tell you that the poore repentant sinner,
Shal be invited to a Heavenly dinner;
And how the wilfull wicked are corrected,
And from Gods favour utterly rejected.
They preach that *pride* shal be consum'd with fire,
And God will raise the *simple* from the mire.
They say that *Envie* is a murthering sinne,
Whil'st *neighbour-love* the love of God dtoh [*sic*] winne.
They teach and proove that *griping Covetousnesse,*
Is cheifest cause of sinne and wickednesse:
Whilst *Charitie* and *fruits* of *Christian love,*
Doth please the *Lord,* and all his *Saints* above.
They say in holy *Scripture* it is found,
That all the world for drunken sinne was drown'd,
And that with water was; but now I thinke,
The greatest part will drowned be in drinke.
They say that *gluttonie* and all excesse,
Shall punisht be in *Hell* with paines endlesse:

[p.31]
27   ***to all Christian Soules.***

And that all *whooredome,* and *adulterous* acts,
All *poisonings, witchcrafts,* and such *wicked* facts,
Treason, perjurie, cousenage, and *lying,*
Unto the *Lord of Hosts* are daily crying.
      And thus they preach the *Law* and *Gospel* too,
And faithfully Gods *holy worke* they doe;
And all to set you in the perfect way,
That *Heaven* may yours be another day.
      By this you see how faire I am within,
Oh blest are *they* that did that worke beginne:
And they that did and doe maintaine the same,
Eternall be their *Honour* and their *Fame*:
But such as seeke that *Glorie* to deface,
Hell be their ende, and in this life disgrace.
      Ah faire *Eliza,* now I thinke on *thee,*
Full foure and fortie yeeres thou succordst me,
And didst defend me with thy *awfull sword,*
'Gainst *proudest foes* that did oppose *Gods word*:
And when away thou must from us be gone,
God and thou send'st a second *Salomon,*
By whom and by whose issue, I am sure,
Paules faithfull doctrine shall with me indure;

[p.32]
28   ***The Complaint of Paules,***

And be maintained, (maugre hellish spite)
So long as *Sunne* and *Moone* doe yeild their light.
His words, *His* workes, *His* will to God is bent,
His bookes doe shew that *Hee* from *God* is sent:
For *Proverbs* to *His Sonne He* did declare,
Then next a *Preachers part He* did not spare,
The third *His song of songs* most sure shall be,
That shall set forth *His Kingly* love to me,
His chiefe delight is all in *Trinitie,*
Of them to make a perfect *Unitie.*
What is the *good* wherein *Hee* hath no part?
What is the *bad He* hates not with *His heart*?
Where are the poore that justly can complaine,
Whose needs He helps not, and their right maintaine?
Where is the *wight* of worth and due desert,
But of *his Royall bountie* hath had part?
And where's the *Princes* that to Him resort,
That doe not of their welcome well report?
And eke extoll His *great magnificence,*
His *wisedome, learning, wit,* and *eloquence*;
As did the *Queene of Saba (Davids sonne,)*
So they admire our *Royall Salomon,*

          1. Basilicon doron.
          2. His Apology for the oath of Allegiance.
          3. Canticum Canticorum.

[p.33]
29   ***to all Christian Soules.***

And say though times doe alter and mens names,
So that our *Salomon* is called J A M E S,
Yet for *his wealth, his wisedome, strength* and all,
A *Second Salomon* you may Him call;
His *Land* the *Israel* that flowes with milke,
And honey sweet, corne, cattell, cloth, and silke,
Gold from all parts, spice, oyle, and wine,
Treasures from East and West, Pearls rich and fine;
People innumerable as the sands,
That well he may send out to forraigne lands,
Great store of them to place and plant elsewhere,
That He an *Israel* new may build and reare,
Whereby *Gods word* throughout the world may goe,
As in the *Scriptures* Christ commanded so:
      Goe yee preach and baptise in every coast,
In'th name of *Father, Sonne,* and *Holy Ghost*:
Which worthy worke his Highnesse hath begunne,
As much as any heretofore hath done:
Virginnia, Sommer-islands, and the rest,
Will testifie in time how they are blest,
By comming of His Subiects there to live,
Which could not be, if He no leave did give.

[p.34]
30   ***The Complaint of Paules,***

By which good meanes those which now *Savage* be,
Will come in time to *Christianitie*;
If not the elder sort, the younger may,
And after one *age* thousands every day.
      Though all things at the first seeme hard to bee,
Yet good beginning have good ends you see,
So it be followed and well protected,
And for *Gods glorie* cheifely be respected;
No such beginnings need to feare good ends,
For they shall have both God and King their friends.
There is not any that for wise would passe,
But holds that *England* as *Virginnia* was,
And how it's now the world may judge with me,
A braver *Kingdome* never eie did see;
            And so (in time) may poore *Virginnia*,
            If seconded by rich *Brittannia*.

The prayer of Paules.

OH God, I pray thee blessee this Royall J A M E S,
Q. ANNE, *Prince* CHARLES, *their issue, & their realmes,*
Prince PALATINE, *and his* ELIZA *faire,*
Their Princely Babe and first borne Sonne and Heire,
Feede *them* with *Manna* from thy *mercie seate,*

[p.35]
31   ***to all Christian Soules.***

Let thy *Word* be their onely *drinke* and *meate:*
Blesse all their *Counsell* (*faithfull, wise, and grave,*)
With every gift good *Counsellors* should have:
Their *gracious* and their *reverend Bishops* all,
Blesse likewise Lord; and more especiall,
Their Rev'rend Kingly Father of this *See,*
Cheife *Lord* and *Preacher* that belongs to me;
Also *their Deane* and *Chapter* of this place,
Blesse with thy loving countenance and grace,
And all the rest of *godly Ministrie,*
And daily them increase and multiply:
Oh make their words and workes for aie agree,
That I the *Halci'on* dayes and houres may see,
Blesse all their *Nobles, Knights,* and *Gentrie* all,
Their *Yeomandry,* and *Commons* great and small.
Blese both their *Nurses* of sweete *learnings* lore,
And all good *Students* now and evemore:
Blesse *Them* from all *designes* of feare and blood,
And from all things that are not for *Their* good:
Poison the poisoners that seeke *Their death,*
And suffer not a *Traytor* once to breath;
Boote out the *Romish rubble* from *their* Land,

[p.36]
32   ***The Complaint of Paules,***

That naught but plots of *murther* have in hand;
Drive farre from *Them* all *Sorcerers* and *Devils,*
And still defend *Them* from pretended evills:
Blowe all the *chaffe* away that spoils good *corne,*
And let no *vaultie villaines* more be borne;
Set markes of *powder-vengeance* in their faces,
And let it there abide to their disgraces.
      Yet Lord, thou art their potter, they the clay,
Thy skill and will can worke them any way:
Then if it bee thy will, for Honour make them,
And in thine anger do not quite forsake them:
Or as the *Scripture* saith, (a *blessed storie*)
Do what thou wilt, *O God,* for thine owne *glorie.*
      Blesse this most *famous Citie* where I stand,
The *Flowre,* the Perle, the Jemme of Brittaine Land,
The Honourable *Major* of the fame,
The *Sherifs* and the *Aldermen* by name,
All other *officers* in *their* degree,
And all good *Citizens* whereso'ere they be.
      My *Benefactors* I doe pray thee blesse,
And frame their hearts to give with willingnesse:
So blesse*, O Lord,* the *Noble English hearts,*

[p.37]
33   ***to all Christian Soules.***

That in *Virginnia* have done *their* parts;
Incourage and increase them evermore,
And still enrich their treasure and their store;
Oh let all *worthie minds* imboldned bee,
To doe the *works* that best may *Honour thee.*
      And I doe pray thee sith the times grow ill,
Teach all the ready way to doe thy will;
So by thy *goodnesse* sinne may be or'e come,
And they prepar'd against the day of doome,
To live with *thee* in thy *eternall* blisse
Where they shall never any comfort misse;
      Unto which blessed place, Lord bring them still,
      That feare thy name and strive to doe thy will.

AND now for to returne where I left off,
Least some perhaps may rashly give a scoffe;
I must complaine of more then yet you see,
Which I desire may well amended bee:
My body round within and eke without,
My windowes, and my pillars all about,
My pavements, and my doores, my leads, my walls,
And many other faults upon you calls,

[p.38]
34   ***The complaint of Paules,***

And craves repaire against all wind and weather,
That wee may give you thanks for altogether.
    The Church the *fæminine gender* doth require,
And like a *Ladies* should bee her attire;
Nay like an *Empresses* adorn'd, and grac'd,
Within, without, in order all things plac'd;
And cheifely that Church which is most insight,
(The head, the members guide, and candle-light;)
So should I bee that all the world may know,
Th'vnfayned love that *Brittaines* hearts do owe
To mee their *Princely Church*, and *Empresse deare*,
In whom the *word of God* doth shine most cleare.
    Say that you should upon your backe bestow
Rich clothing, as ther's many doe I know,
And on your head a threedbare cap should weare,
Motheaten, and at ev'ry touch to teare;
Would you not thinke that all which see you goe,
Could chuse but wonder why you should doe so?
In all whatsoever like to like is best,
If one part be well cloth'd, so let the rest;
Or els that which is base makes all seeme base,
And by that fault doth all the rest disgrace.

[p.39]
35   ***to all Christian Soules.***

    Were it not strange also (*oh pardon mee,*)
That any one within the *Court* should see
Our *Royall Queene* attir'd in base aray,
And all her hand-maides cloth'd in garments gay?
I thinke t'were strange, and such unseemely sport,
As never will (I hope) be in our *Court:*
    Yet even so the case with mee doth stand,
That am the *Queene of Churches* in this *Land:*
For in the middle of a matchlesse *Citie,*
I stand like to a *mourner,* more the pittie,
Invironed with buildings faire about,
And I am tallest built in all the rowt;
All other *Churches* are but *dwarfes* to mee,
Yet unto all beare-headed must I bee;
My head should weare the *Crowne* full well I know,
But that must stand upon the toppe of *Bowe*:*
Or els the shaft or spire that should bee best,
But that's upon S. *Dunftanes* in the *East;*
My chime of fine small bells might well be heard,
All London over, but I am afeard
That some will say, what need such cost be there?
Because (of chimes) there be enough elsewhere:

* Bowe steeple in Cheapside verie well beautified at the cost of one
Parish.

[p.40]
36   ***The complaint of Paules,***

But such *Lobiectors* I could wish were dead,
That better minds might come in place and stead;
Let such hoard up for *Sir Hugh Prodigall,*
Or *Sir Raph Want-wit,* you may *noddie* call,
Whose backe and belly cheere, *Tobacco* smoake,
All *good designes* doth hinder, stifle, choake.
    Some few (I hope) the Lord will ever raise,
To bee the *light* and *mirrour* of these dayes,
That (in good time) will pittie my complaint,
And with my wants will all my friends acquaint,
And stirre them up tp be as *franke* to me,
As God (to them) is *bountifall* and free.
    One such a *Sutton* as of late did die,
That turned *Charter-house* to *charitie,*
If to himselfe the *honour* he would have,
With halfe that charge he might repaire me brave ;
But such a worthy *Phoenix* is so rare,
That hardly any will with him compare;
Nay would tenne thousand would now joyne in one,
To doe as much as he alone hath done.
    But stay a while (my *Muse*) no further goe,
What is the reason thou art grieved so?

[p.41]
37   ***to all Christian Soules.***

Let not fell anger in thy heart take place,
But patiently I pray thee, beare a space;
Not any of my coate should angry bee,
But gentle, mild, and full of curtesie;
Nor should *beggers,* (men doe say) bee choosers,
Least craving all, they still are all the loosers.
    I thinke now on a good conceit and true,
That doth my comforts once againe renue;
For listning what the *Princes* said of late,
(When *they* were pleas'd to be on my bald pate,)
As I did understand this was *their* talke,
As *they* (about) on ev'ry side did walke;
Alas good *Paul* (saith one) how poore and bare,
Thy head, thy sides, thy battlements now are?
Is't possible that long thou shouldest thus stand,
In such a *Cittie* and a *prosperous* land?
As I am *Christian* I'le speake for thee,
That once againe thou mayst *tryumphant* bee:
Thy shaft shall up againe, thy cocke shall crowe,
Or else thou shalt be *crown'd* as well as Bow:
Which of these two will surest on thee stand,
I will entreat thou maiest have out of hand:

[p.42]
38   ***The Complaint of Paules,***

Comfort thy selfe (*good Paul*) be not dismaid,
It shalbe done to thee, as I have said;
To which the other *Princes* all agree'd,
And said it should bee surely done with speed.

  THIS did I heare, or els was much deceiv'd,
And of my sence of hearing quite bereav'd;
But that's no marveile if it so should bee,
For age, and cold, breeds much infirmitie,
And waiting so long bearehead is a thing
That (to the soundest) may diseases bring,
And make him so benummed, and so weake,
That hee shall hardly stand, or heare, or speake.
Indeed I am or'ejoy'd, I must confesse,
When I am visited with *Princely* guests;
For then I hope, some good will come to mee,
Towards releife of my necessitie;
So joy might make me to mistake *their* speech,
Which (if I did) I humbly doe beseech
A pardon for this fault, and then hereafter
Ile write of nothing but Ile bring mine Author,
To verifie the truth of that I write,
Or els my pen shall never more indite.

[p.43]
39   ***to all Christian Soules.***

  And for my *Writer* also let me crave,
His pardon likewise I would gladly have:
His learning you may see is poore and weake,
And I can make but signes, I cannot speake;
I shew'd my coate, my head, my broken sight,
How poore it was, how bald and wanting light:
Whereat he vow'd, that he would never rest
Untill with state and beautie I were drest;
For which I must not shewe my selfe ingrate,
But pray that he may live right fortunate:
His meaning's good, that you may plainely see,
Though he want *Eloquence* to polish me,
Beare with his wants, accept of his good will,
Encourage him that is well minded still.

  If once I were attired faire and brave,
Then London all her ornaments shall have;
All things would then be sutable to me,
And to my friends most gratefull will I bee:
For then will I when my Request is done,
Send to the banks of learned *Helicon*,
Or to *Pernassus mount*, where *Eloquence*
Doth passe my Authors dull intelligence,

[p.44]
40   ***The Complaint of Paules,***

Where I shall finde such fruits on Eden tree,
As shall set forth their favours done to mee;
And on my *Pinnacles* there shall they place,
Most thankefull *mottoes* for my *Founders grace.*
And more to shewe their loves and good intents,
They shall set *poesies* on my *battlements*,
That shall my *Benefactors* love unfold,
To all the world in sentences of gold.

  Let't not be said when you for Christ his sake
Warre with his enemies doe undertake,
That your *religion* doth with Church decay,
But let your seene, your unseene *zeale* display;
That valiantly you may your selves expresse,
Like *Christians* stout in *weale* or in *distresse,*
In spight of all that wicked wights can doe,
And for the glorie of the *Gospel* too.

  Then famous *Brittaine* thou'lt be happie still,
In godly pleasures thou shalt take thy fill:
Feare thou no *foes* for *Christ* will be thy guard,
Whose *breath* can make a mightie *host* afeard:
Thy *Kingly David* also can dispute
With Turke or Antichrist, and them confute;

[p.45]
41   ***to all Christian Soules.***

And when to *warres his Highnesse* shall incline,
He'le quell the *pride* of stoutest *Philistine*,
And in the meane time with a *Bible-stone*,
Will dash his braines, and crush his greatest bone:
For he that in his breast doth weare that *sheild*,
(As doth this *Dauid*) needs not feare the field:
But with true *faith* and courage *he* may meete
Sathan himselfe, and stampe him at his feete.

  His golden pen that wrote for *Christ* his sake,
The *Angels* up to *Heaven* did it take;
And bid *Him* be as bold with *Pike* as *Pen,*
For He should be the onely *King* of men,
And that in *Him* and *His* posteritie,
Should be or'ethrowne all *Popish heresie:*
Which Christ (I pray thee) grant it may be so,
To all that *Thy* just quarrell undergo:
  For sweet's that BLOOD *that in Thy cause is shedde,*
  As was Thy BLOOD *that Thou for man hast bledde.*

  And now for to conclude what hath beene said,
I doe beseech my *povertie* be wai'd:
Oh let not base *Oblivion* burie me,

[p.46]
42   ***The complaint of Paules***

Least in *Oblivion* I doe burie thee,
And scorne that thou shouldst build within my *wombe,*
To grace thy selfe with any sumptuous tombe,
Where thy remembrance must indure for aye,
And I poore Church be suffered to decay.
My *Innocence* pleads no such *Ignorance:*
But if I were dispos'd to cast a glaunce,
I soone could finde such costs on *tombes* laid out,
As almost would amend me round about:
These in my bowels neere my heart must lie,
And I poore ragged wretch must pitie crie:
And this the purse of ten or twelve have done,
Yet left enough for wife, and every sonne.
      Can tenne or twelve doe so, and twice as much?
And shall a *citie* and a *Kingdome* grutch
To give a trifle to so good a deed,
As should releeve my povertie and neede?
And not so given, neither as quite lost,
For that were vanitie and idle cost;
For from thee it doth goe unto thy brother,
(I meane the workeman, and to many other.)
      That's cast away, that goes out of the Land,

[p.47]
43   *to all Christian Soules.*

And comes no more in *King* or *Subjects* hand:
Or that that's hidden in the earth, or bagges,
While thy poore Brother's naked, or in ragges.
      Oh come with gladnes then unto this charge,
Brittaine is wealthy, populous, and large,
And those that give in love and charitie,
Into a *Booke* let them recorded bee,
That childrens children may hereafter know,
The love their *fore-fathers* to me did owe:
And be incourage'd in their younger dayes,
To doe the works deserving lasting praise:
      for he that doth deferre good deeds till death,
      Seild comes to good the thing hee doth bequeath.

ON bended knees of *love* and *loyaltie,*
And at the feete of *Soveraigne Majestie,*
King, Queene, and Prince, and Privie Counsellers,
Archbishops, Bishops, Brittaines Senators ,
Once more I doe most humbly, begge and crave,
That my defaults amendment now may have:
Nobles, Knights, Gentrie, Commons great and small,
In *love* and *reverence* I pray you all,

[p.48]
44   ***The Complaint of Paules, &c.***

That ye these faults will helpe for to amend,
For *Brittaines honour* till the world doth end:
Wives, and *Widdowes, Maidens dying, living,*
Unto this worke of *Pietie* be giving;
According to your works yee shall inherit,
Yet for your works no place in Heaven can merit:
For what is he that since the world beganne,
Hath beene so just, and so upright a man,
Whose good works could exceede above his evill,
But onely *Hee* that conquer'd death and devill?
That Christ, that Lambe, that Dove, that God-man, he
Did onely merit your eternitie.
      To him therefore doe you his praises send,
      And so of my Complaint I make an ende.

Laus Deo in æternum.

[p.49]
45

THE EPILOGUE:

OR,
An Extasie, which Paules *fell into*
after it had complained : partly of Hope, and
partly of Feare.

W H E N my complaint was ended, I amazd
Stood, and beheld how people on me gazd:
My thought that every one that walked by,
Did looke upon me with compassions eie:

E X C E P T some twelve, and that was *Envie* one,   1
A pale-fac'd fellow, wishing good to none :
He vo'wd, and swore from his more gall then heart,
Unto my need he would no penny part:
      His reason beeing asked, he replied,
      All others but his owne good he defied.

[p.50]
46   ***The Epilogue.***

2   T*HE* second was a *miserable* Chuffe,
      Hee at at my mournefull suite did storme and puffe:
      And said, for all my povertie and ragges,
      He would not part with money from his bagges.
         Shall I (said hee) give any thing to thee,
         If I should want, what canst thou give to me ?
3   T*HE* third was *Pride,* and he did looke so hie,
      That he could not my povertie espie :

> To give (he said) it is not now the fashion;
> And for to beg, it's held abhomination.
4   THE fourth was *Carelesnesse;* his answer was,
> That for my need and wants he did not passe,
> His reason why he will no bountie give,
> Is cause (quoth he) I'le stand while he shall live,
>> And so departs with scoffing, and with laughter,
>> And bids them care that ought to care hereafter.
5   THEN *Pickthanke* comes, the fift he is in number,
> He pries in others faults, and makes great cumber,
> And for to save himselfe from any charge,
> He doth not care how he doth speake at large,
> And reckons up collections made before,
>> (Inough for to releife my wants and more:)

[p.51]
47   ***The Epilogue.***

So that if others were i'th minde hee's in,
He would see that before he would beginne.
> *Alas,* if such a thing were done before,
Let it not now be laid on good mens score;
Whose wills are such (although they are not many)
Me to repaire without the helpe of any:
>> But sith their meanes compareth not with minde,
>> (Without some helpe) I can no comfort finde.
>> THEN *Curiositie* the sixt goes by,
>>   6

And cause he sees a moate in's brothers eie,
(A word amisse, a syllable, or such,)
To give a shilling therefore he doth grutch:
And thus he peepes, and pries, and lookes asquint,
And thinks that beggers words should be past print:
>> When (God doth know) if he were charitable,
>> The plainest tearmes should serve if he were able.
>> THE seaventh, *Prodigalitie* that asse,   7
(That by Duke *Humphry* oft doth hungry passe,)
He saies, Tobacco, Claret wine, and Sacke
He will not want, though twentie Churches lacke;
To playes and playing, taylor, or to launder,
Or for a toy, he cares not how he squander:

[p.52]
48   ***The Epilogue.***

But when poore *Vertue* doth but crave a groate,
He's ready in his wrath to cut her throat.
8   THEN comes the eight, (*Haile master*) with his traine,
> Hee saies, what need such wast? it is but vaine:
> It had beene better given unto the poore,
> That beg about the streets from doore to doore:
>> But such a *Judas* (if he beare the bagge,)
>> Hath no intent the poore should have a ragge.
9   THE ninth I take it was a *Jesuite,*
>> (For I did heare him mumble words of spite)

And swore by all the blacke deeds he intended,
> He'd rather hang then I should bee amended:
> Hang then (quoth I,) or get thee going further,
> For thy delight's in ruine and in murther:
> Thy curse can doe no harme, thy blesse no good,
> Nor all such villaines as delight in blood:
> For God in holy *Scripture* hath appointed,
> That none should hurt his *Church* or his *Anointed:*
> Therefore avant thou wolfe in lambskins cloath'd,
> For through the world thy acts and deeds are loath'd.
10   THEN comes the tenth an *Atheist,* not an *Ar'in,*
> (Though both I do esteeme as dung or carrin;)

[p.53]
49   ***The Epilogue.***
He vext and storm'd that any Church should bee
Where *Soules* should worship any *Deitie:*
> A man to seeme he was, but not Gods creature,
> Because he held all things proceed by nature.
> THE leaventh was a *brother* seeming pure,   11
That no good works will heare of or indure,
And all the comfort which to mee he faith,
That I (Asse hee,) must stand and live by saith;
> By faith (quoth I,) what faith dost thou live by?
By faith it's good when in good faith you lie;
If I had not a *Faith,* more sure, more humble,
I soone should crake, and rent, and fall, and tumble:
> Wherefore be gone (*Prophane*) thy *faith* deceaves,
> And all the world of *charitie* bereaves.
> THE twelv'th and last, a clouted shooe did weare,
>   12

The surest foun-
dation of Pauls
is the Church
under it called
S. Faith.

And in his hand a hedging bill did beare:
(I meane the *wretched man,* that is so cruell,
That makes his mucke, his Idoll and his Juell,)
He saies and sweares, (and yet he prates and lies)
That all his wealth's not worth two apple pies;
When (if he were) to take a goodly varme,

Or in some spite to doe his neighbour harme,

[p.54]
50   ***The Epilogue.***
His Jugge and hee agree both in one zound,
And from their hutch can vetch a hunderd pound:
> And yet he pines and pules for doing good,
> As if in povertie and want he stood.
And thus with griefe of mind, and in some fury,
I have impaneld up my unkind *Jewe-ry,*
Whose *verdict* would be such if they may speake.
As would my heads, and heart for sorrow breake.
> *But* now these unkind *twelve* are gone and past,
Twelve hundred thousand I espie at last,
Virtues welwillers men of charity,
Such as doe pray for my prosperity.

They say I may without be decked brave,
Yet in my inward parts no *pride* may have;
I may have *earerings*, *corronets*, and *laces*,
I may have *lovers*, *kisses*, and *imbraces*;
I may have *Honour* due unto a *Queene*,
And all this while no *pride* in mee is seene:
I may have any thing to make me faire,
That all *truths* lovers may to mee repaire,
And bee enamor'd at my lovely face,
And strive who most can enter to my grace.

[p.55]
51   **The Epilogue.**

Not as the wicked money-changing-rout,
(In time of prayer) walke my Isles about,
And make their bargaines, and their idle meetings,
With many false, and fayned newes, and greetings:
    But as my friends in fervent *zeale* and motion,
Come for to heare Gods word with sound devotion ;
My thinks they looke, and smile, and speake, and give,
And wish that I triumphantly might live;
They doe not seeke for faults, as others doe,
But doe good deeds, and yet are faithfull too:
They sound no trumpets when they give their almes,
They have in them no peevish froward qualmes;
But all in *love* and *dove-like charitie*
They give, and give in Christian veritie:
    Wherefore (as is my duty) I will pray
    That *God* will blesse them all both night and day.

[p.56]
52

THE DREAME.

─────────────────────────

ON the one and twenti'th day,
Of the pleasant moneth of *May,*
To a grove I did repare,
All alone to take the aire;
Sweete it was, and fresh, and greene,
Decked like a *Summer Queene:*
Where abiding privately,
I did here fine melodie:
Philomel did chaunt and sing,
Welcomming the cheerefull spring:
Every bird did straine her throate,
Warbling out her pretie note.
    Walking there a little space,
At last I went with nimble trace,
To a river somewhat neere,
That had water pure and cleere:
Fishes there did leape and play,
Swannes did sing their roundelay.

[p.57]
53
So I set me downe to rest,
In a place that lik't me best;
And beeing there a little while,
Slumber did mine eies beguile
Till at last a sleepe did take me,
That no noise till night could wake mee:
The place was sure, and I was bold,
The aire was pure, not hot nor cold:
My pillowes were greene grasse and flowers,
The willowes were my shadie bowres;
My little dogge did so attend mee,
That no creature could offend mee.
    In this sleepe (good Christian people,)
I dreamed of a Church and steeple,
Which at first my thought was bare,
As many other ruines are,
Weather-beaten and much worne,
Rag'd, deformed, crackt, and torne
Without battlement or grace,
Too too meane for such a place:
For my thought this Church did stand,
In the best citie of this land,

[p.58]
54
And for seate and eminence,
Had the cheife preheminence:
Wondrous great it was in sight,
And of admirable height:
King and people might it see,
How it was in pouvertie:
And all strangers well might say,
'Twere pittie it should so decay,
Where Gods word is well regarded,
And his Preachers are rewarded.
    In this dreame (though fast I slept)
Yet (with teares) I truly wept,
And did pray that God would blesse,
Such as would this Church redresse.
    After teares were over-past,
Joy did visite me at last,
For my thought this Church was mended,
And the steeple was befriended.
    Fashions many I did see,
Er'e any fashion pleased me;
One as before (a seemely spire)
Which was burned downe with fire,

[p.59]
55
One like *Pulchres*, one like *Bowe*,
One like *Boston* was I trowe;

One *Grantham*-like I did espie,
But his toppe stood not awry:
And many other I did see,
In this dreaming fantasie;
But that which seemed to be best,
Followes after all the rest,
Which if your pleasure be to read,
You'l say it was the best indeede.
    My thought the steeple was ta'ne downe,
Lower then the Churches crowne,
And suddenly was rais'd againe,
With good labour not in vaine:
Square it was as t'was before,
Twelve foote higher t'was and more;
Round the toppe a *battlement*,
Seemely, faire, and excellent;
Above that *battlement* full high,
Foure pinacles I did espie,
Hollow, and of stone so sure,
That till doomes day would endure:

[p.60]
56
On the toppe of every one,
Was a little spire of stone,
At the feete whereof there went,
A little pretty *battlement*:
Round about these *battlements*
Were fine *phanes* and *ornaments*,
By whose motion without stay
Drove the crowes and kites away:
In each *phane* was guilt the *Coate*
Of *benefactors* of best note;
And in a place convenient,
On th'infide of each battlement.
A *poesie* thus was set in gold,
As underneath you may behold;
    All glorie be to God on hie,
    And to this Church prosperitie.
These pinacles foure *pictures* had,
Which to see did make me glad;
That which stood next to the West,
Had his face towards the East;
Looking with maiesticke grace,
For to see his Saviours face;

[p.61]
57
A *King* he was, a *Crowne* he wore,
God blesse him now and evermore:
For sure as *London* hath a *Thames*,
It was the picture of *King James*:
His *Armes* were in the highest phane,
And then many noble man,

Had their *Armes* under *His*,
Round that *battlement* I wisse:
Like to *spangles* they did show,
Unto such as were below;
And they that did to th'toppe resort,
Might say it did belong to'th Court:
His *Kingly motto* there was plac'd,
Which the *Pinacle* most grac'd:
    Evill come to ill intenders
    Good to all true Faiths Defenders.

___

    THEN I lookt to that i'the *East*,
Where a *Bishop* was at least,
Opposite unto the *King*,
Which to me much joy did bring;
In one hand he had a *Booke*,

[p.62]
58
Wherein he seemed for to looke,
In a sweete and rev'rend wise,
Well beseeming such a guise:
His other hand did touch *his* tongue,
And a *sentence* thus he sung;
    To my Saviour Ile be true,
    And this Church shall have her due,
On the toppe his *Scutchion* stood,
Which to see it did mee good;
Under that were all others,
Which by calling were his *brothers*:
    This *Pinacle* did plainely show
The *rev'rend Bishops* did it owe,
And the *Clergie* with them joynd,
Because they would not be behind.

___

Then I saw towards the North,
Another *pinnacle* of worth;
Where was sitting in a *chaire*,
One resembling a *Lord Mayor*;
The *Cittie Armes* were highest there,
Under that all *Citties* were:

[p.63]
59
A *Shippe* was carved there also,
As if thee on the *Sea* did goe:
Then a *motto* there was set.
Which the Citie grace did get:
    Walworth killed rebell Straw,
    Cause he spurn'd 'gainst King and Law;
    So by our truth and industrie,
    God makes our Citie multiply:
    Let rebels swagger how they will,
    We will bee true and loyall still.

This *pinacle* belongs to'th'Citie,
The *motto* is more true then wittie.

_____

THEN to the South I turn'd mine eie,
And in that Pinacle did spie
A *Country-man* the plough to hold,
A comely Farmer somewhat old,
A *Wheat-Sheafe* was his *Armes* I trowe;
And the rest that stood belowe,
Were implements of husbandrie,
Set in the *phanes* most handsomely:
And his *motto* thus was fram'd,

[p.64]
68
As here underneath is nam'd:
    Plaine I am as you may see,
    Yet the Best growe rich by me.

_____

TWIXT each *Pinacle* there was,
Pyramides that did surpasse,
For beautie and for seemely forme,
Strong enough for any storme.
    In the middle of each square,
There they stood and placed were.
    One had the picture of a *Queene*,
The fairest that mine eyes have seene,
Who surely as I'm honest man,
Seem'd to be our *Royall Anne*:
For it had such Maiestie,
Ioyn'd with *gentle clemencie*,
That certainely it was the same,
Which before I seem'd to name.
    Her motto on the same was set,
Which I never shall forget:
    Faire without, and grace within,
    Are beauties fit for Church and Queene.
And the poesie generall,

[p.65]
69
Which I named first of all,
There was placed in degree,
As high as all the others be:
    All glorie be to God on high, &c.

_____

THE second *Pyramides* had,
The picture of a *royall Lad*,
Which I imagin'd ever since,
Did resemble *Charles* our Prince,
By each part of limme and feature,
He did seeme a *Kingly creature*;
Stout and bold, gentle, free,
And all that in good *princes* bee:

His motto now I will set forth,
Cause it was a thing of worth:
    I scorne the feare of shedding blood,
    For God, for Church, for Countries good;
    But for all these Ile warre and fight,
    As Kings and Princes should by right:
    I will helpe the poore oppressed,
    And those which truly are distressed.

[p.66]
62
THE third as faire as was the rest,
With *Elizabeth* was blest,
Rhynes sweete *Princesse, Brittaines joy,*
Holding in her armes a *Boy*,
Whom (if Art doe not dissemble)
Her first borne He did resemble.
    At which sight I was amazd,
And with joy on them I gazd,
Ravished with admiration
At this delectable fashion,
Thinking if such great delight,
Could be in the *pictures* sight;
What would then the substance bee,
Unto him that may them see:
I am sure to me t'was Treasure
For to see them in this measure.
    Her motto now I will declare,
Kill me, if the same I spare:
    In the Churches wealth and peace,
    Good things prosper and increase:
    But if shee wither and decay,
    All Gods blessings fleete away.

[p.67]
63
In the fourth faire *Pyramide*,
Two other *Pictures* I espide,
One of *Denmarks royall King,*
Whose fame with us shall ever ring,
And shall be linked in this knot,
Where *He* shall never be forgot:
Three *Queenes* in one is *His Sister*,
Twice in *England* hath he kist *her*,
With such great joy on all parts,
As pleas'd ten hundred thousand hearts.
    His motto was as doth ensue,
Beleeve me it is very true;
    I Christian King of Denmark, give
    My love to These, while I doe live,
    And will assist with power and sword,
    My kinred, friends, the Church, Gods word.

_____

By him was Prince *Palatine*,
Looking on *his Valentine*;
Each to other seem'd to glance,
With a cheerefull countenance,
In such an amiable sort,

[p.68]
72
As my soule did therein sport;
    This *Prince a Motto* did unfold;
Fit and worthie to be told:
    Gods spouse and mine I will maintaine,
So long as I do live and raigne,
Turke, Pope, nor devill, shall them fright,
Or do them hurt by day or night,
And in this Gordian knot will I
Bee knit in love untill I die.

    THEN in the middle of the *square*
Where all these brave pictures were,
There was rais'd (tenne foote higher)
A *curious* and a *costly spire:*
And at the top thereof a *Crosse*
Of Silver guilt and not of drosse;
Then a gallant cocke to showe,
Which way still the wind did blow;
    In this place good *Art* was tride,
How to make it sure abide,
And accordingly t'was fram'd,
That no workman could be blam'd;

[p.69]
73
Not too weightie nor too light,
Like *Cheape-crosse* it was in sight,
But the *pictures* there that stood,
Were of *Princes* that were good,
That this *Church* did er'st advance,
And gave it store of maintenance.
And first the lowest placed there,
Elizabeth and *Henry were*,
One of proofe one of hope,
Better *Princes Heavens cope*
Ever had or ever can,
Be better amongst the sonnes of man:
Then betwixt them I espide,
Two *Princesses* that lately di'd,
Which looked like those of *King Iames*,
Gotten since *hee* dwelt by *Thames*.
    And above in the next round,
Other *Princes* there I found,
Pictur'd all in their degree,
As by time now dead they bee:
There in letters of pure gold,
Their right names I did behold:

[p.70]
66
And I thinke in hollow brasse,
Ev'ry *picture* shaped was.
    This *spire* was hollow, and with lead
Round about t'was covered;
Fram'd with oken timber pure,
Such as ever will endure:
    In that hollow was nought els,
But a score of little bells,
Which the *Art* of wittie times
Made a delectable chymes:
Who being high, their prettie sound
Might be heard the Cittie round.
    In the midst of th'upper loft,
A paire of wodden stayres were wrought,
And a doore at that stayres head,
Which did bring mee to the lead;
Where my thought I did behold,
All that I before have told.
    As about the leads I went,
And saw all things so excellent,
Looking over, I did see
The *Church* likewise as it should be,

[p.71]
67
With new *battlements* about,
And walls mended throughout;
All the windowes where need was,
Were amended with pure glasse:
Not anything that wanted there,
But was repaired ev'ry where,
Never did I see a thing,
Of more worth and reckoning,
Then this *vision* which I
In my sleepe did plaine espie.
    Had I beene an *Architect*,
Dreaming of this faire prospect,
Or with true tearmes could relate,
All the fashion, forme, and state,
Then might I say it taught mee more
Than any practise did before;
But many things of note and worth,
I am not able to set forth.
    After long I had beheld
The outward beautie if did yeld,
Then I was upon the pinne,
To see what *Grace* it had within;

[p.72]
68
Downe I went, (my thought in hast,)
But my speede did prove in wast:

For (to mee) it's griefe to tell;
I was waked by a bell,
And my dogge beganne to bay,
At a frogge leapt crosse my way,
By which meanes I did not see,
How the same within might bee;
And more worse (to end my theame)
It vexed mee t'was but a dreame;
Well I wisht the Sexton hang'd
And my dogge I soundly bang'd:
Yet to give them both their right
T'was time to goe for it was night,
And I thinke my foolish curre
Knew t'was fit for me to stirre:
So away I runne in hast,
And came safely home at last:
Where with pen I did record
All I dreamed word by word:
And I hope it's not amisse,
To place it where it placed is.

[p.73]
69
THUS you see (good people all)
What is done for *Londons Paul*;
If in ought my *Dreame* proove true,
Let it be as't pleaseth you:
Though I dreame I doe not teach,
That's a straine beyond my reach;
Since I lear'd my *Crosse rowe* letters,
I left all teaching to my *betters*;
And leave it will unto my ende,
So good *Reader* be my friend.

The Booke to Paules.

According as you doe command,
I will flie about the Land,
To Court, Clergie, Countrie, Citie,
For to find out Ladie Pitie:
If I finde Her *and returne me,*
Pray take order none may burne me:
Though I be but poore and plaine,
I may bring you store of gaine:
For this Ladie *doth not care,*
(In pious uses) what shee spare;

[p.74]
70

The Dreame

To the Church shee is more free
Then thousands other Ladies bee.

The answer of Paules.

BOOKE I thanke thee for thy *love*,
And do pray to *God* above,
Thou maist finde this *Lady* out,
Where thou goest round about;
That thou maist returne againe,
With a labour not in vaine.
    For thy burning take no care,
Thou wilt surely better fare;
I will keepe thee in record,
Till the coming of the Lord.
    And thy Author here shall rest,
    Whilst his soule with God is blest.

F I N I S.

APPENDIX 2

[p.1]

Portland-Stone

IN

Paules-Church-yard.

Their Birth, their Mirth, their Thanke-
fulnesse, their Advertisement.

Written

By HEN: FARLEY,

a Free-man of *London:*

Who hath done as freely for Free-Stone,
within these eight yeares, as most
men, and knowes as much of their
mindes as any Man.

Buy, or goe by.

LONDON,

Printed by G. E. for R. M. and are to be
sold at the great South doore of
of Pauls, 1622

[p.2] blank

[p.3]

THE AUTHORS
CHARGE TO HIS
BOOKE.

TO know where *Portland* is,
    If any doe desire,
Left they should thinke amisse
    Tell them in *Dorsetshire.*

[p.4]

The Authors charge to his Booke.

For some perhaps will say,
    That doe not understand
From whence they be, that they
    Came from a forraigne Land.

So *England* may have wrongs,
    And eke a noble *County,*
And God to whom belongs
    All thanks for his great bounty.

[p.5]

The Authors charge to his Booke.

For sure as Hee's above,
    Then we, no living Nation
E're tasted of his love
    In more abundant fashion ;

Of things which named be
    Above or underground:
Or on, or in the Sea
    That can or may be found.

[p.6]

The Authors charge, &c.

His name be blest therefore :
    And so my Booke adieu,
I need to say no more,
    But pray God prosper you.

[p.7]

The Bookes answer.

Your Charge I will obey
    As I am bound by right :
And what y'ave writ I'le say
    To Lady, Lord, and Knight.

In hope though I am weake,
    And in proportion small,
Yet so y'ave taught me speake ,
    As some good doe I shall .

61

[p.8]

The Bookes anfwer.

And workmen will take heed
To doe what's just and fit,
Which is as much as need,
Where Conscience is and Wit.

[p.9]

TO THE RIGHT
Honourable, Reverend,

Worshipfull, and worthy Commissioners, appointed by the Kings
most Sacred Majefty, for the Reparation of S[t]. *P A V L S* Church
in L O N D O N:

My very good Lords and Masters.

IF *your grave Wisedomes*

herein I offend.

My faithfull Muse

did never so intend ;

For (though but plaine)

shee's honest, and shee's true,

And hath respect to God, King, Church and You.

[p.10]

The Epistle

In all humilitie shee's well content,
For her least fault to be right penitent ;
And (of your favors) craves but this for guerdon,
If well, your boon; if ill, your gentle pardon.

Amore, Veritate, & Reverentia.

So devoted to Gods House,
And to your Lordships and Worships
ever bounden,

H E N :   F A R L E Y.

[p.11]

T O   T H E   R I G H T
Reverend Father in G O D,

G E O R G E , Lord Bishop of

London, &c. My singular
good Lord.

AS from the Hill
of *Hermons* Heav'nly tops,
Most Sacred Dewe
on *Sion* Mountaines drops :
Which falling further to the lower ground,
Doth make the Fields with *fruits divine* abound;

[p.12]

So may that *Hermon Dewe* be dropping still,
On thee (*chiefe Montaigne*) of *Pauls-Sion* Hill;
That so Her lower grounds may fruitfull be,
And She (*poor Church*) made fortunate by Thee
For which I pray, these Blessings may ensue,
Health, Plenty, Peace, Joy, and Long-life to You.

H. F.

[p.13]

This is no Nettle, thorne or thistle,
But unto Envy an Epistle.

PE*rhaps you doe delight to flout and fleere,*
Perhaps a word may be misplaced here,
Perhaps some thing may touch you very neere,
Perhaps you doe beleeve, your threats I feare,
Perhaps you love me not, the case is cleare,
Perhaps you doe backbite me every where,
Perhaps you thinke it comes not to mine eare,
Perhaps you crost my new bookes sale last yeare,

[p.14]

Perhaps you know I cannot quit this geare.
Yes, if I would as envious appeare :
But what need I, sith acting thus your part,
You wound your selves (by Envy) to the heart.

H. F.

[p.15]

PORTLAND
STONE IN
Pauls Church-yard.

E'Re since the Architect
    of Heavens faire frame,
Did make the World,
    and Man to use the same ;
In Earths wide wombe,
    as in our nat'rall bed,
We have beene hid,
    conceal'd, and covered,

[p.16]

Portland Stone in Pauls Church-yard.

Where many thousand ships, have sailed by,
But knew us not, and therefore let us lye.
    Till at the last, and very lately too,
(Some Builders having building worke to doe,
And time be'ing come we could no longer tarry,
But must be borne from out our earthly quarry)
We were discover'd, and to *London* sent,
And by good Artists tryde incontinent :
    Who (finding us in all things firme & sound,
Fairer and greater then else-where are found ;
Fitter for cariage, and more sure for weather,
Then *Oxford, Ancaster,* or *Beerstone* eyther,

[p.17]

Did well approve our worth above them All,
Unto the *King* for service at *White-hall :*
    Where being quickly come, as quickly we,
Had welcome to his *Sacred Majesty,*
And (for our humblenesse full many a day)
Were still exalted highest every way,
In workes of most perspicuous Eminence,
Which in all buildings have preheminence :
    As *Columnes, Cornish, Capitals,* and *Basis,*
In *Fillets, Frise,* in *Ornaments* and *Facis,*
In *Architraves,* in *Pedistals,* and *Pillars,*
And (as the onely best of our well-willers)

[p.18]

Portland Stone in Pauls Church-yard.

His Highnesse now our service doth preferre
Unto the Church, to joyne and dwell with Her:
    So that from one good *Montaigne* to another,
And from our *Mother-earth,* to this *Church-mother*
We come apace, and are preparing aye,
To cure her evils, and her great decay ;
To be her front, her bulwarke, and defence,
And also to renue her excellence.
Where Hymnes and Haleluiahs shall be sung,
With praises to the Lord by old and young,
From day to day, and so from yeare to yeare,
Till Christ his second comming doth appeare.

[p.19]

O happy age, wherein such things are done,
Thrice happy we that now may see the Sunne,
And be united to this sacred place,
(A grace to us beyond all other grace)
For thus wee know the truth of truest story,
All that God made, he made for his owne glory;
And at one time or other come to light,
To doe man service, and their Maker right,
That very senslesse things may him adore,
And magnifie his holy Name therefore.
O Blessed God preserve our Royall *James,*
honor his name among the honor'd names

[p.20]

Portland Stone in Pauls Church-yard.

    Of best procedent Kings that ever stood,
Renown'd for Wisedome, and for doing good :
Make him a second *Salomon,* a peerlese Jemme,
In these his Kingdomes, this his *Jerusalem :*
Lengthen his dayes, his treasure still increase,
And let him live, and dye, a King of peace,
    So blesse, O Lord, our high & mighty *Charles,*
And then the names of Barons, Peers and Earles,
The worthy Knights, and Gentry of this Land,
That to this Worke doe set their helping hand.
The Bishops, Clergy, Citie, Country, All,
(And as our duties binde in speciall)

[p.21]

This Rev'rend Bifhop for his love to us,
Let him be famous as M A U R I T I U S,

Anno 1087. This Church of Saint Paul was much wast-
ed by fire; and worthy *Mauritius* here mentioned (then
Bishop of *London,*) beganne a new foundation thereof,
in manner as now it is, upon Arches and Vaults of
stone, for defence of fire. In which worke he continued a constant and a bountifull Benefactor for 20 yeares together, and then dyed. After him (viz) *Anno* 1107
succeeded Bishop Beaumais, who won-
derfully encreased the same Church for 20 yeares
more, pur-chasing at his owne costs the large Streets
and Lanes round about it, which he beganne to com-
passe above with a strong wall of stone, and Gates.

[p.22]

Portland Stone in Pauls Church-yard.

Long liv'd as *Nestor,* and in every way
Happy and prosperous till his dying day ;
That still he may this famous Church advance,
In gaining her both Coine and Countenance,
Till such a noble Register be seene
Of Benefactors, as hath never beene
In any age or any worke before,
And till he say, *Enough, there needs no more.*

    And cause no mourning in our streets may be,
With such as feare demolishment to see.
Lord for thy Names sake, let it be thy pleasure,
The rather to encrease that pious Treasure,

[p.23]

That every one may have some satisfaction,
To gaine their prayers in so good an action,
And that two Noble workes together may
Be bravely done, to all true Subjects joy;
And through the world this fame may ever ring,
Pitty did raigne in Bishop, Lord, and King ;
Mercy and Justice were so met in one,
That Justice (scarce) from Mercy could be knowne.
    So, for a Nation pittifull and loyall,
Great Britaine shall winne praise past all deniall.
No man shall need to grieue, or to lament,
For's place of Custome, or Demolishment :

[p.24]

Portland Stone in Pauls Church-yard.

And blessings many will the Worke attend,
From the beginning to the very end,
    But yet, though pitty here we doe request,
That none may thinke themselves too much opprest,
Let such as must depart their houses know
No winde so calme or warme did ever blow,
Nor ever was a Worke so good as this,
But that with some it blew or went amisse.
    Then sith herein the wind blowes somwhat ill
For such as joyne to *Pauls* against her will ;
That have impair'd her strength by vaults & cellars
To make more roome for Buyers and for Sellers,

[p.25]

Let them with patience endure some losse,
And for the Worke sake beare a little crosse;
Not grudgingly, or by pronouncing wrong,
Cause ther's their Custom, there they lived long
For though desire of gaine's a grievous Tempest
There is a Proverb bids them *Caveat Emptor.*
And ne'rethelesse their Custome and their trade,
This House of God must new againe be made.
    Was it not example scurrilous and rude,
At first to grant that trades should there intrude ?
Nay are they not accursed, that did yeeld
To make Gods Court a merchandizing field ?

[p.26]

Portland Stone in Pauls Church-yard

May we not call them beasts, even to their faces,
That like bruit beasts defile such sacred places ?
Things consecrated unto Pious uses,
Is't fit that they should suffer foule abuses?
Is there no civill difference or ods,
Twixt cleane and unclean things, mans house & Gods
Shold *Christians bones* be dig'd out of their graves
And laid with dogs bones in the fields by knaves,
That so more roome under the Church foundation
May be for *A-iaxe* in a beastly fashion?
No easment but again the Temple wals?
No other place to pisse, or make Laystals?

[p.27]

No way to passe with burthens, but throgh *Pauls*
wher burthend consciences shold ease their soules?
And 'cause she is materiall, as men tearme her,
Is it materiall therefore they should harme her?
 Looke well about thee Reader, and then see
Whether such things as these ought so to be:
And after due consideration had, then tell
If therewithall God can be pleased well:
Or if there doe belong no curse or woe,
To such as first gave way to wrong her so:
Or if it were a credit to our Nation,
At all to grant so base a toleration:

[p.28]

Portland Stone in Pauls Church-yard.

For we doe know thou wilt agree with us,
To hold it vile and sacrilegious :
And all good men that after looke upon her,
Will say, 'tis to this Land a great dishonor.
 O that we had such gifts of tongue and pen,
As there is given to some sonnes of Men ;
That by perswasive reasons we might winne
Th'abusers of Gods house to know their sinne:
That with their Soules they might no longer flatter
But understand it is a haynous matter ;
And will be punished before mens eyes,
When all things wronged shall in judgment rise

[p.29]

But we are blockish yet, not past our letters,
And (being divine) we leave it to our Betters.

So now you Workmen, listen what we say,
(You are so call'd by work, and not by play)
If ever you were Masters of your Trade,
Make this best Master-peece that ere you made
'Tis for the Church, and therefore doe not spare
Your best advice, skill, diligence and care :
And as (some wayes) you stand on reputation,
So labour now to get the commendation :

[p.30]

Portland Stone in Pauls Church-yard.

Not for precedency, lest then you erre,
For all's one here, both Free and Forreyner ;
And as she doth receive all sorts to prayer,
So any Worke-man, any good Surveyor,
She may retaine to gaine her Reparation,
As for the Church is us'd in every Nation.
And yet we hold it were both sinne and pitty
Sith Work-men live in this renowned Citie,
Good Artists, honest, paying scot and lot,
If more then others they should be forgot ;
But rather be preferr'd in some degree
Before a Stranger, whatsoe're he be.

[p.31]

And 'cause our Writer a poore Free-man is,
We hope these words no man can take amisse;
For what he write's according to his oath,
Which to infringe we know he will be loath;
That is, the Cities honor to maintaine,
And also to advance Her honest gaine.
 So once againe we doe revive our Muse,
And to all workmen doe more counsell use ;
Learne by the Scriptures what you ought to doe
Let them direct your hands and conscience to,
Ezra, Ne'miah, Chronicles and *Kings*,
And *Haggai* will shew you many things :

[p.32]

Portland Stone in Pauls Church-yard.

How justly men did worke about the Temple,
Which there is Registred for your example ;
And with what joy and love they did proceed,
The Booke of God will shew you if you reade:
For happy was that man that could devise
Most curious worke to grace that Edifice :
Or hee whose purse or person could present
Ought that might help to make Her excellent.
Lead, timber, stone, brasse, iron, some men gave;
Some lyme, some sand, some glasse, to make her brave
And Laborers, like Bees, did labor truly,
Observing all their times and houres most duly.

[p.33]

    Then if your owne gaine you doe only plod,
You are unworthy for the House of God;
For if you worke by taske-worke, or by day,
Your pay shall be as just as ere was pay;
And therefore 'tis expected you should bee
Not sparing in your worke, but francke and free.
    Some men there are will maintain to ones face,
(But such we hold both lewd and very base)
That in a worke for King or Church they may
Trifle the time by loytring and delay.
    Some will be working hard, but when doe thinke
Just when they have no coine, or trust for drinke;

[p.34]

    Portland Stone in Pauls Church-yard.

———————————————————

Or when the Clocke is neare the stroke eleven,
And say they have so wrought e're since 'twas seven,
Or when some Officer they doe espie,
That otherwise cashiers them presently.
    Some with their Rules do sidle up and downe,
As if they did more worke then all the towne :
But mark them wel, & give them their due check
For one weeks work, almost three daies they lack
    Some spend much time in finding fault, and so
To picke a thanke will nimbly runne or goe.
Till at the last, the seed which they have sowne,
Brings forth a fruit more fit to be their owne.

[p.35]

Some have the gift of working more then some,
Untill a holiday, or Sunday come.
But then what they have got six dayes before,
They will consume it, if 'twere ten times more :
Mean while poor wives & children live ful bare
Hoping when husbands come of better fare,
And they returne when all the worke is done
As poore as *Job*, or as the *Unthrift Sonne*.
    Some have their jobs to doe in other places,
And so they worke like *Janus* with two faces ;
And from that taske that longest will remaine,
They oftentimes an houre or two will gaine.

[p.36]

    Portland Stone in Pauls Church-yard

———————————————————

But hee that in this worke proves such a Jobber,
Is but a kinde of Sacrilegious Robber.
    Others, at every one that by them walke,
Will to their fellowes have some thing to talke;
& while their tongues are tatling, 'tis their course
To hold their hands, and that is ten times worse.
    So there are other some that for a need,
When hempe is scarce, will onely buy gape-seed,
And looke about as if nought were their taske,
But for to answer all that men will aske,
And thinke it is a colour fit t'excuse
The precious time they wrongfully abuse.

[p.37]

These, like some Schollers that are sent to schools
Have a good conscience, though not little fooles;
And make *Pauls-worke,* the Proverb true doth stand,
Of every little thing they take in hand :
With whom to live a faithfull Clarke ath 'works,
As good goe dwell with Saracens and Turkes.
But now we thinke no man will be so rude.
    And thus in charitie wee doe conclude.

             F I N I S.

[p.38] blank

[p.39]

    Pauls merrily,
      yet modestly.

———————————————————

IF *Preachers now will speake for me,*
In Parish Churches where they be,
And all good hearts agree in one,
Then farewell my Complaint and moane.

Our good King James, *he hath begunne,*
And eke Prince Charles *his onely Sonne :*
With many a Noble Lord and Peere,
To give me money every yeere.

[p.40]

O follow such brave Leaders then,
All you brave-minded English-men :
For what you give it is not lost,
But brings a blessing for your cost.

So Portland *stone sith you are come,*
To joyne with me till day of doome,
Untill that day we will be friends,
And wish them good that good intends.

[p.41]

Certaine Additions of the Author,
as they were given to the King and
Prince, in the Parliament-time last, and
at the Christmas following

CHrist the Beloved of the King of Kings,
A pparant Heire of Heav'ns rich Diadem ;
R ejoyce the Heart, and Spirit as all things,
O f this faire Branch of our most Royall Steward,
L ong Life good Wife, (faire ladie) give to Him,
U nto His present Age and day of Birth,
S end Him all Blessings both of Heav'n & Earth.

P Rotect Him by thy Power Omnipotent,
R enowne Him in the Court of Parliament,
I nstruct Him by thy Wisdome from above,
N ever be absent from Him in thy Love;
C rowne Him with Triumphs and great victories,
E ver confound (or turne) His Enemies;
P rosper His going out, and comming in,
S ave Him in all assaults of deadly Sin.

Amen.

[p.42]

IN sixteene hundred *Twenty one,*
(A yeare you may remember)
Prince Charles was aged *Twenty one*
The Nineteenth of November,
The Nineteenth yeare of J A M E S *our King*
His peacefull happy Raigne :
God blesse Them both, and Their Offspring,
Till *S H I L O* come againe.

He that did write for Pauls *(nam'd Henry Farley)*
Prayes thus for Them, and so will late and early.

F I N I S.